Contents

Acknowledgements		2
1	Once Upon a Time, in the Depths of Mysterious Arabia…	2
2	First Saudi Rashidi War, 1902–1909	16
3	Emergence of the Ikhwan, 1910–1914	25
4	The Great War, 1914–1918	33
5	First Saudi-Hashemite War, 1918–1919	61
6	Kuwait-Nejd War, 1918–1920	64
7	Conquest of Asir, 1920–1923	65
8	The End of the Rashidi Emirate, 1920–1921	67
Bibliography		70
Notes		70
About the Author		74

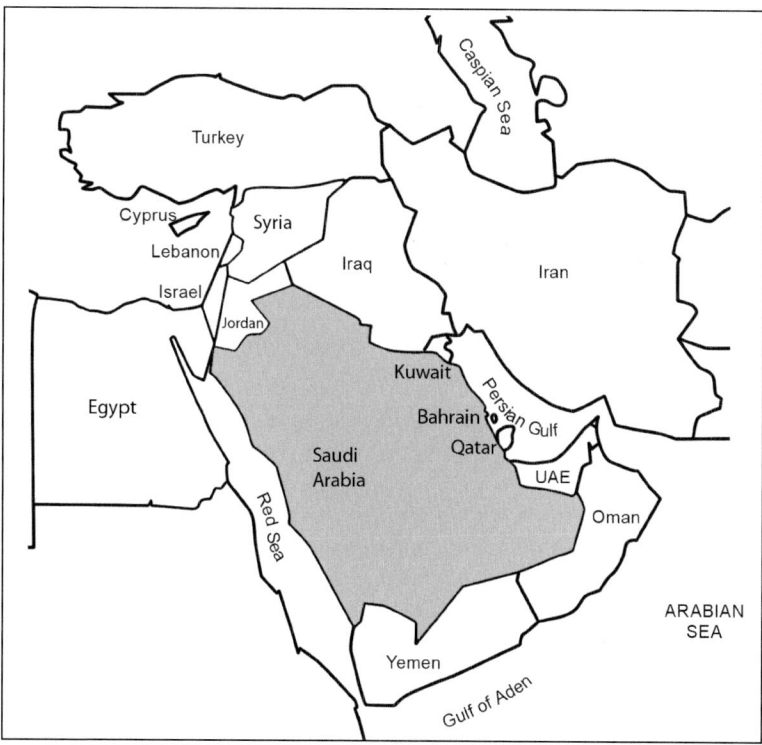

NOTE

In order to simplify the use of this book, all names, locations and geographic designations are as provided in *The Times World Atlas*, or other traditionally accepted major sources of reference, as of the time of described events. Arabic names are romanised and transcripted rather than transliterated. For example: the definite article al- before words starting with 'sun letters' is given as pronounced instead of simply as al- (which is the usual practice for non-Arabic speakers in most English-language literature and media). Instead of using the diacritical marks to represent the letter *'ayn*, double a is used, and names like 'Faisal/Feisal' are spelled using the commonly preferred English language variant – 'Faisal', likewise other names included in the text: 'Hussein', 'Hashemite' and 'Sheikh'.

COVER

A mounted warrior of the Saud tribe, armed with a Damascene sword, against the backdrop of the holy Well of Zamzam (*Bir Zamzam*), within the Masjid al-Haram, the Great Mosque of Mecca. (Artwork by Renato Dalmaso)

Helion & Company Limited
Unit 8 Amherst Business Centre, Budbrooke Road, Warwick CV34 5WE, England
Tel. 01926 499 619
Email: info@helion.co.uk Website: www.helion.co.uk Twitter: @helionbooks Visit our blog http://blog.helion.co.uk/

Published by Helion & Company 2025
Designed and typeset by Mach 3 Solutions (www.mach3solutions.co.uk)
Cover designed by Paul Hewitt, Battlefield Design (www.battlefield-design.co.uk)

Text © Javier G. de Gabiola, with Tom Cooper 2025
Color profiles: Renato Dalmaso, Luca Canossa and Tom Cooper 2025
Maps drawn by George Anderson © Helion & Company 2025

Every reasonable effort has been made to trace copyright holders and to obtain their permission for the use of copyright material. The author and publisher apologise for any errors or omissions in this work, and would be grateful if notified of any corrections that should be incorporated in future reprints or editions of this book.

ISBN 978-1-804518-73-1

British Library Cataloguing-in-Publication Data.
A catalogue record for this book is available from the British Library.

All rights reserved. No part of this publication may be reproduced, stored in a retrieval system, or transmitted, in any form, or by any means, electronic, mechanical, photocopying, recording or otherwise, without the express written consent of Helion & Company Limited.

For details of other military history titles published by Helion & Company Limited contact the above address, or visit our website: http://www.helion.co.uk. We always welcome receiving book proposals from prospective authors.

ACKNOWLEDGEMENTS

To my wife, Carolina Martínez Zamora, and to my daughters María, Alicia and Carolina for their support and patience in helping me complete this paper during the holidays in Puerto de Mazarrón, Murcia, in August 2023.

Also, I would like to thank Tim Barger, from Sellwa Press, for kindly providing the original maps from Sander's book in high resolution, and to Mesut Uyar for his information about the Ottoman armies around 1908-1911.

1

ONCE UPON A TIME, IN THE DEPTHS OF MYSTERIOUS ARABIA…

On the black night of January 15, 1902, just six days after the end of the holy month of Ramadan, and illuminated only by the shy smile of the rising moon, fifty-three men waited hidden in a palm grove north of Riyadh. The Wahhabi faith had turned the city into a convent, where everyone was asleep and there were no parties or music. Twenty-three Bedouins broke away from the main group, and advanced between the irrigation canals and gardens until they reached the cemetery, on the north side of the city. This they crossed stealthily. They carried a trunk of a palm tree that served as a scaling device. This improvised device was left resting on the crumbling city wall, at a stretch of this ruined fortification that barely reached half of the normal 25 feet (8 meters) in height. Nine of them nimbly climbed, led by a giant, a tall and strong young man, barely 26 years old, who despite his size ascended with the agility of a feline. This was Abdulaziz ibn Abd El-Rahman al Saud, or Prince ibn Saud, known by his followers as 'The Leopard'. Next to him was his cousin, Abdullah ibn Jiluwi, and together they would try to recover the ancestral capital of the Sauds, now in the hands of their enemies, the Rashidi, who had about 80 men there to defend it.

Ibn Saud had left his half-brother Mohammed behind with the camels and thirty men. With the rest of his force he moved on the *Mismak*, or citadel. The home of the Rashidi governor, Ajlan, was near the Mismak too. Because the Sauds did not exactly know which building was his home, they approached to the only house with lattice windows. To be sure they were correct, they knocked on the door of another nearby house inhabited by an acquaintance of theirs. When the servant opened up, the intruders entered and interrogated him: one way to gain access to Ajlan's house was to go over the rooftops, crossing those of neighbouring houses until reaching that of the governor's. Saud nimbly passed from house to house, followed by his men, and entered Ajlan's harem. There, after locking up the women, he and his men were, as tradition required, served with tea and dates, a relief as they had been riding for 60 kilometres without eating. In cold blood, they waited until the dawn, the time when Ajlan would return to his residence from the Mismak. During the wait, the rest of his men managed to join ibn Saud – all except those of Mohammed's group.

As the Sun rose, ibn Saud listened to the noise of the heavy gates of the Mismak open, from there he saw Ajlan coming out with an escort of six men – still sleepy but armed with swords. The Prince did not hold back, and in a fit of fury he shouted: "*I will kill you, come on, akhu Nura!*" (I am Nura's brother). Running downstairs, he charged at Ajlan, followed by his warriors. Ajlan struggled to get out of his padded blue winter cloak with red edges, but managed to strike out with his sword, a strike that Saud was barely able to stop by blocking with his rifle. Ajlan fled to the Mismak, but it had

Abdulaziz ibn Abd El-Rahman al Saud, or ibn Saud, known as 'The Leopard', in his first known picture, taken in 1910 when he was 34 years old by his friend Captain Shakespear. (photo by Shakespear, Royal Geographic Society, via Sander)

already closed its door behind him. Saud shot at Ajlan several times, wounding him in the shoulder and forcing him to drop his sword. One of Ajlan's guards engaged and held off two Saudi warriors, but a third cut the guard's throat. In the meantime, Ajlan had managed to run until reaching the postern, a little gate, near a window, on the

The Riyadh walls in 1917, deteriorated and surrounded with palm trees, probably as seen by ibn Saud in 1902, too. (Photo by Philby, 1922, Frank Cass, via Sander)

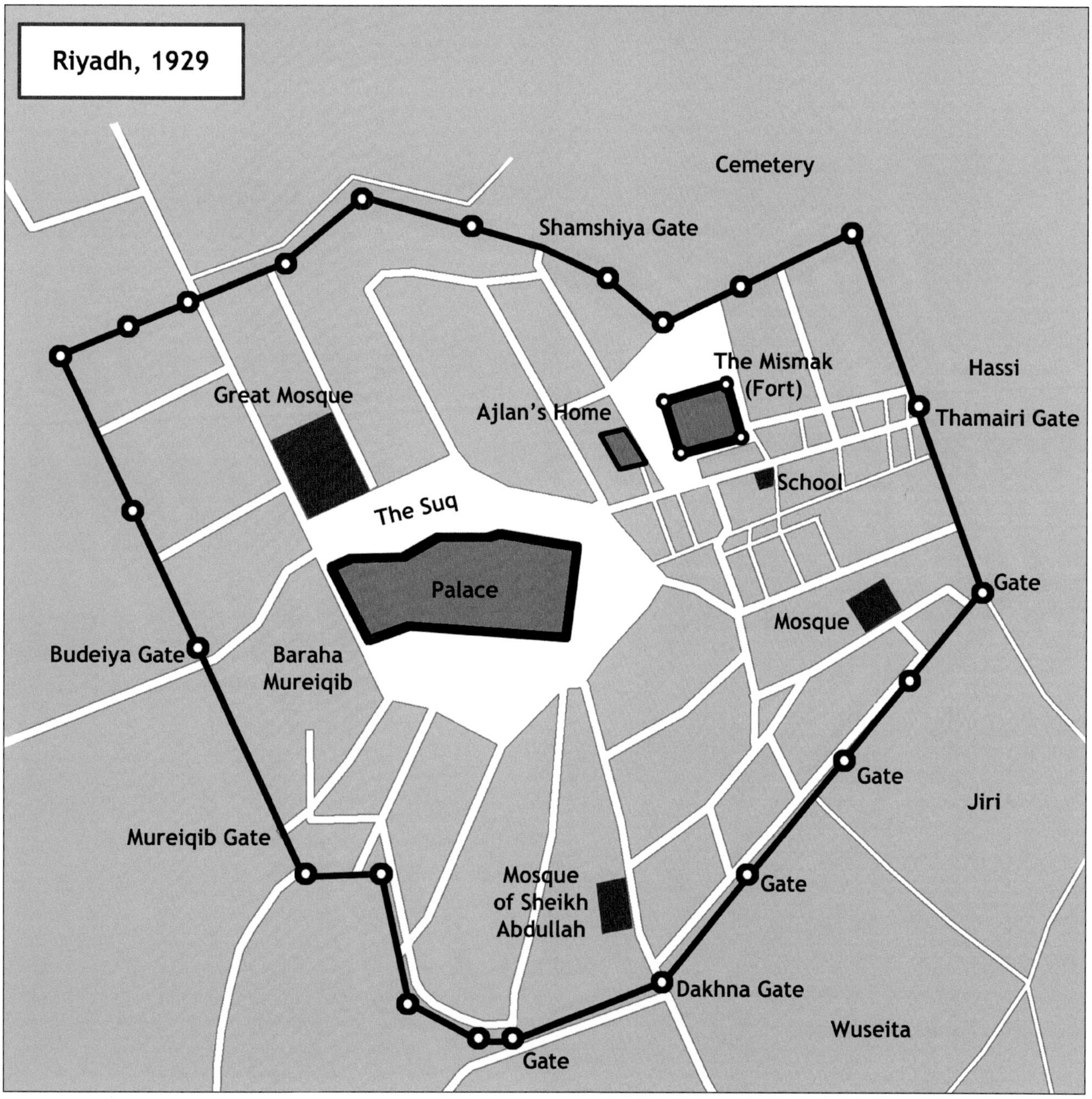

Map of Riyadh drafted by Philby in 1922. It shows all the major places of Saud's surprise attack: Ajlan's house, the Mismak, the Cemetery, etc. (Map by Tom Cooper based on a draft by Philby, 1928, via Sander)

The Fort Mismak (or citadel), Riyadh, where Rashidi governor Ajlan was attacked and killed by ibn Saud. (De Gaury, 1946, via Sander)

The postern or little gate (de-facto a window) through which governor Ajlan tried to escape followed by ibn Jiluwi and ibn Saud. The soldier points to the place where ibn Jiluwi's spear almost killed Ajlan (De Gaury, 1946, via Sander)

right side of the main door of the Mismak, and he tried to crouch down to enter it. Ibn Saud caught up with Ajlan, grabbed him and threw him to the ground. Fighting for his life, Ajlan kicked Saud in the groin, making him double over in pain, and jumped back to the gate, this time he managed to get through. A spear thrown by ibn Jiluwi struck near him, but missed, nailing itself to the right of the postern. ibn Jiluwi, without thinking and without knowing what awaited him on the other side, ran headlong through the postern, followed by Saud himself. The guardians of Ajlan were by this time already fleeing, leaving behind their governor: wounded, he could not follow them.

Now, inside the Mismak, the Sauds removed the iron bar from the main gate of the fort, enabling 21 other followers to follow them. They entered the guardroom, killing everyone who resisted, while Jiluwi caught Ajlan and finished him off. In the end, after an hour of fighting, eight Rashidis were killed or wounded, for six Sauds, two of them killed. Triumphant, ibn Saud climbed the battlements of the Mismak and threw Ajlan's head into the street, shouting: *"Who is with me? Who? Your Amir is with you again!"*[1]

ARABIA, AN 'EMPTY LAND'

For the majority of citizens of the Kingdom of Saudi Arabia, this is how they believe the history of their nation began. The action by ibn Saud and his two dozens of followers in the shadows of the night was the initial chapter of a story that would change the destiny of the Middle East forever, giving rise to the birth of a new nation: the Arabia of the Sauds. As an omen, the day ibn Saud retook Riyadh was also his birthday. What better a present than this?

For the majority of the outside world, this story is entirely unknown, something that took place in some forgotten corner of the World. On the contrary, many may argue, the contemporary history of the Middle East begins with a British Army officer named Thomas E Lawrence – famous as 'Lawrence of Arabia' – travelling to Arab Peninsula in 1916, to 'spark' an 'Arab revolt against the Ottoman rule' – and memorably portrayed by Peter O'Toole, in David Lean's 1962 eponymously named movie.

Ibn Jiluwi, ibn Saud's cousin who killed governor Ajlan in combat. Hard and very strict, mainly with the Shi'a, he would fight the Rashidis and then, later, serve as the governor of al-Hasa in 1913. He was devastated by the death of his son during the civil war in 1929. (Unknown photographer, via Sander)

In reality, by 1916, there was long history of Western travellers visiting the holy sites of Mecca and Medina on the Arab Peninsula dating several centuries back, and the British hardly had to spark any kind of an uprising against the Ottomans. Indeed, an 'inter-Arab' war had been raging already for hundreds of years; the region already had a history of numerous and bloody wars with the Ottoman Empire, and a major emerging local power was already in a de-facto state of war with the Sultan in Constantinople (re-named Istanbul in 1930). Similarly, for the majority of the locals, the British were no 'neutral observers' that mysteriously 'suddenly appeared on the scene', but were already well-known as – alongside the Ottomans – another major outside power, all the while lurking, waiting for an opportunity to impose their will on the region. The core reason for the actual, on-going situation was that the Arab Peninsula of 1916 was in the process of a major development: the unification of the majority of Arab tribes living there.

To fully understand the difficulties and the achievement of that unification, it is necessary to take a closer look at the local geography. The area of modern-day Saudi Arabia is 2,149,690 square kilometres. It is a giant country - the length of all of Western Europe, and more than four times the size of France or Spain, or 10 times that of the United Kingdom. The local geography appears to be an infinite space: empty, almost flat, devoid of water and without great geographical features. This emptiness makes it only possible to orient oneself by the position of the sun and the stars. In truth, apart from several groups of hills, the only relevant ground relief in this region are the Uads, Uadis, Oaudis, Waadis or Wadis (its pronunciation depending the local language or dialect, and/or whether Spanish, French or English): these are dry river beds that cross the earth as trenches, and that only from time to time are filled with water, forming torrents during the scarce spring rains season. To the north beyond Arabia, at the level of Palestine, Lebanon, Jordan and Syria, there is a large coastal extension of Mediterranean climate, similar to that of Spain or Greece, about 160km deep. Beyond this distance the humidity of the sea disappears. The rains are almost non-existent, and become everything in the almost barren land. Agriculture is impossible until 800km inland and the cultivated valleys of the Euphrates and the Tigris rivers.

Farther south, in Arabia itself, there is no such coastal Mediterranean climate, and the desert reaches the very shores of the Persian Gulf and the Red Sea. On the southern coast, between Yemen and Oman, the climate is milder because the monsoons from India arrive in these lands. Any exception to this harsh climate, therefore, is located outside what would become the future borders of Saudi Arabia: it an immense desert. However, to the experienced eye of an Arab there are quite a few distinguishing features in the geography of this barren land. The most commonly known desert type (and the most terrible), the one full of sand dunes, is actually the scarcest in Arabia. It practically only exists in a couple of places: a strip (widened at the centre) in northern Arabia, the Great *Nefud*, *Nefood* or *Nafud*; and the Rub' al-Khali, or 'Empty Quarter', so called because it is totally empty except for the sand. This is a huge rectangle of sand of 650,000 square kilometres: that is larger than France or Spain, and it covers the eastern border to Yemen, all of Oman, the United Arab Emirates and Qatar. For this reason, it acted as a geographical barrier that ibn Saud was unable to cross and could not conquer these regions. The Great Nefud to the north, and Rub' al-Khali to the south, are linked by two or three tongues of sand that run east and west of Riyadh, the Dhana. These are so narrow that they can be crossed in just a day or two, so they do not constitute an insurmountable barrier. All of this desert, sand and dunes, is unproductive and deadly.

The other, more extended deserts in Arabia are, incredibly, able to support certain crops cultivated in a certain way, in certain places and under certain conditions. These other deserts, formed by limestone rock and rolling hills, despite the scarce rainfall, are enough for the appearance of some thickets. In winter and spring even, some ground is covered with herbs and flowers, this being a source of food for livestock of sheep, goat, camel and even horse. And inside this 'desert' there is an isolated area in central-eastern Arabia, called the *Nejd*, *Nejed* or *Najd*, where there are oases, cities and cultivated areas, centred around Riyadh, Qasim (somewhat farther north) and Shammar (even farther north, the house of the Rashidi), which is where the richest heart of agriculture in Arabia is located. This area was abundant in water springs and underground wells, unlike other

Wadi Ruhm, in the area dominated by the Howeitat tribe, near the present day frontier between Saudi Arabia and Jordan – a good example of the typical Arabian desert. (via Muphy)

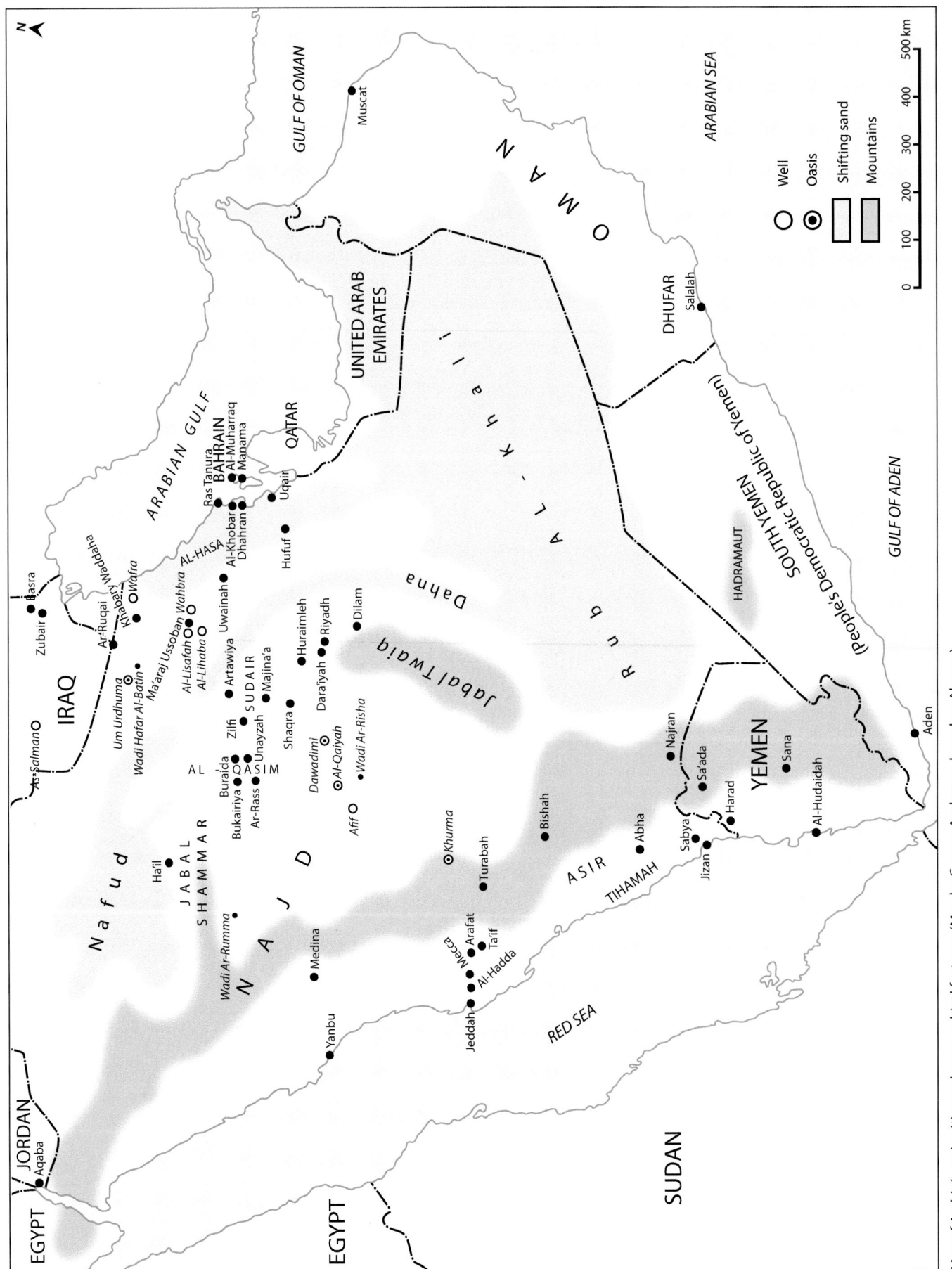

Map of Arabia's main cities and geographical features. (Map by George Anderson, based on Almana)

areas. That being said, these lands are like an archipelago of oases and cities totally surrounded by an ocean of desert, and without continuous expanses of crops. Travellers, caravans, and armies would have to survive without food and water on hand for several days before reaching the next oasis. This desert is like the open sea, and the oases are like the ports in which to take refuge.²

NOMADIC AND SEDENTARY TRIBES

Thus, in Arabia there are three types of desert: that of sand, a dead land; that of earth and rock, which allows growth to feed livestock; and that of the oases of the Nejd, which allows certain crops and human settlement. Therefore, there are also two types of settlers: sedentary people, who are inhabitants of cities and oases; and nomads, who wander with their livestock in search of pasture. In July, nomads can be in the arable areas, but in autumn, the farmers of the oases cultivate the fields, so that the nomads, mainly the Bedouins, cannot graze there with their livestock and have to leave these lands in around October and November. However, as during this time the rain begins to fall in the desert, the Bedouins go there following the rain and water with their herds, only to return again in July to the arable lands of oases and cities, when the harvest is already finished. In the desert, the vegetation is almost non-existent, but, ironically, because its territory is so large there are always areas with enough pasture for livestock that once exhausted, after a few days, merely moving a dozen kilometres farther makes it possible to find another area of pasture. As a result, between winter and spring shepherds and Bedouins are constantly on the move.

Only between summer and autumn do both nomadic and sedentary communities coexist. On the one hand, during this time, nomads sell their livestock, wool and milk to farmers and traders. In

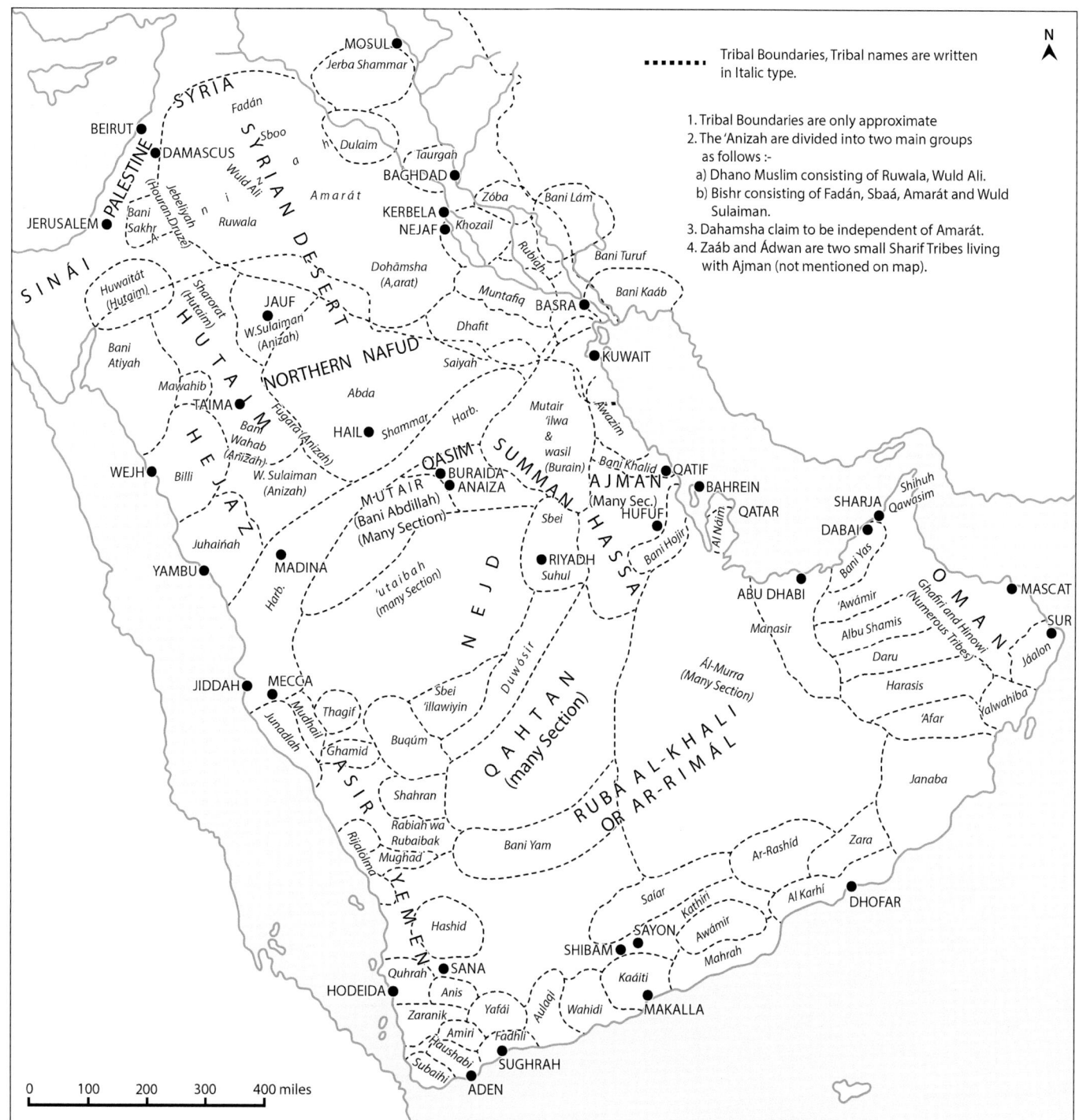

Map of main tribes of the Arabian Peninsula and Mesopotamia. (Map by George Anderson, based on Dickson and Sander)

turn, they buy clothes and other products from the cities so they can survive the rest of the year with their families. On the other hand, the only source of income for the Bedouins throughout the year occurs during these stays in the cities in the autumn. The income is very scarce: a dozen camels for sale per family, but they will only sell one or two, at 15 or 20 GBP each. With that money they will have to buy everything they need to survive later in the desert. Therefore, the Bedouins are forced to practice stealing to survive, constantly joining warlike expeditions to obtain booty. This practice was not carried out against members of one's own tribe, but against those of neighbouring tribes. Therefore, it was extremely difficult to unite different tribes for a greater cause, such as the expansion of the kingdom or Wahhabism. Most tribes were at odds with each other through continuous clashes and robberies, and the law of Talion prevented cooperation between them. Ibn Saud understood this limitation after a few years and would break this vicious circle by practicing forgiveness. Later, there came a time when, with the creation of a modern state, these plundering activities were no longer allowed, which caused the extinction of the Bedouin way of life.[3]

BEDOUINS, SHEPHERDS AND MERCHANTS

The Bedouins had some interesting character traits. Having to survive in such a hostile environment, friendship was of supreme value due to the dependence they had on other people in order to live. Thus, in the face of an enemy the Bedouin lacked mercy, but with friends they were even willing to give their lives for them. In the same way, hospitality towards travellers was sacred since a Bedouin did not know when he himself would be in a position to ask for help from a stranger to survive. In addition, this hospitality was also the only way to find out what was happening in the world, or in the other confines of the desert. John Bagot Glubb – also known as Glubb Pasha and Abu Hunaik in modern-day Jordan, a British military officer who served in Iraq in the 1920s, and then led the Transjordan's Arab Legion from 1939 to 1956 – recounted how in his experience in the desert, it was surprising to observe how the Bedouins knew exactly at all times where this or that tribe or some armies were. The Iraqi officials of urban origin were unaware of, or despised this source of information, as did their British supervisors. However, Glubb immediately understood how this information system worked among the Bedouins, and always placed a table with tea or coffee outside the entrance of his open tent, inviting any traveller who passed by to share the table and from where, in conversation, he was able to ask for and learn all the rumours and news of the desert.

The Bedouin way of life was tremendously austere. Their constant need to move prevented them from having any kind of furniture, making them all sit on the floor and therefore all at the same height, subtly removing social barriers. Similarly, the sizes of the tents to accommodate family were limited by their portability, so there were no major differences between one tent and another. The tribes – divided into sections if they were very large, such as the 'Ataibas – were the grouping together of Bedouins with a common ancestor, and were the axis of the nomad's life. In Glubb's words, "*they were not only his country, but also his trade union, his club, his insurance*

Wadi Ithm, another good example of the Arabian desert: some dry trees but enough food for the camels. The armed Bedouins are part of the Lawrence's expedition against the Port of Aqaba, during the Great War. (via Murphy)

Hashemite Bedouin camp, during the Great War, a good example of the Bedouin camps. (Pierre Perrin, via Desperta Ferro)

policy and his retirement pension." That is why ibn Saud would have a hard time breaking intratribal solidarity to replace it with intertribal solidarity in the form of the Saudi State, based on the same, Arab language and the same religion: Wahhabism.

A Bedouin´s life was not very intellectual. As they were often in solitude, with nothing to do in the desert except wait, Bedouins were very contemplative. They used to talk about death, which always haunted them, and about the meaning of life and religion. Their way of being was simple, plain, and direct, like the horizontal line of the desert that accompanied them throughout their lives. Their treatment of others was often rude; they could be difficult to deal with since they were arrogant. They gave more importance to the pursuit of personal glory than to material achievement or comfort: an example of this being once they obtained what was necessary to feed their family, the rest used to be distributed among their friends or among the people they welcomed as hospitality.

The Bedouins were not the only desert nomads, however. Sheep and goat herders roamed too, and lived separately from Bedouins because their cattle were incompatible with Bedouin cattle. Camels can march quickly and without water through large areas of the desert, with their owners mounted on them; just a few bushes are enough for food. On the contrary, sheep go slower, in flocks, with their owners on foot, and they need more water and grass to feed. Generally, the shepherds were ancient Bedouins who abandoned their customs to avoid the harshness of the desert and live closer to the cities. Shepherds were more civilized, and, in fact, they were much richer than the Bedouins because the inhabitants of the cities always bought their sheep, and in large quantities. The shepherds did share some traits with the Bedouin, such as living in tents and nomadism, but they lacked their warrior skill. Furthermore, they often travelled separately, or in small groups of few families, so that they were the easiest prey for the Bedouins.

Another interesting prey for the Bedouins were merchants. Merchants used to buy rice, flour, tea, coffee, sugar and clothes in Egypt, Palestine, Syria, Iraq and the Gulf states. They would transport them in caravans through Central Arabia to sell in the different cities of the Nejd. Merchants were not as good fighters as the Bedouins, but they were more distinguished than them and also had developed combat experience, having to defend themselves in groups from looters' attacks. In this, they resembled the inhabitants of the cities, who although less accustomed to war, were nevertheless more reliable when it came to obeying orders, forming a kind of urban militia similar to that of medieval cities. As a result, city inhabitants were more accustomed to fighting in groups and did not give up the fight for looting, but, on the other hand, they were reluctant to march far away from their homes on campaign.[4]

THE ARAB ART OF WAR

The way the Arabs waged war, with the differences already commented on between Bedouins, Shepherds, Merchants of caravans and citizen militia, was based on looting and was quite bloodless. Elders, women, and children were always respected, and their aim was not to kill the men (unless there was an outstanding score between them), but to drive them out and away so that they could steal at will, especially the livestock flocks of sheep and camels. Therefore, although they were brave and very skilled in war, they were individualistic and unreliable for a commander, since they tended to avoid a clash if it was going to be bloody (for example in the instance of a frontal attack), and often left the battlefield in the middle of the fight to loot the enemy camp. In addition, they

Ibn Saud's servants preparing his food using one yard wide cauldrons to be filled with lamb and rice. (Sander, 1939)

A detailed view of a Hashemite Bedouin warrior during the Great War. (Photoaisa, 269334, Mary Evans Collection, via Desperta Ferro)

used to release prisoners, who were well treated, and even gave them provisions for the way back to their tribe.

Although they also had warhorses, most of their mounts were camels which unsuitable for hand-to-hand combat, barely for an initial charge, and impossible to aim from with a rifle, due to their constant swinging and movement. Therefore, the Bedouins used to ride by camel and then dismount and fight on foot, forming a tenuous line of warriors who shot their rifles glued to the ground, like a troop of dragoons. This bloodless and non-violent way of waging war clashed terribly with the arrival of the fanatical Ikhwan. These murdered all men except babies, and sometimes also women and girls, driven by their religious zeal 'to cleanse Arabia of the wicked'. Moreover, the Ikhwan, hoping for Paradise, did not avoid the head-on clash and fought to the death. With capable leadership, therefore, they became a formidable war machine.

In looting parties, and especially with the Ikhwan, an apparently peaceful vanguard was sent alone to locate and spy on potential prey, gathering information from them by availing themselves of the hospitality of the unaware, spied upon tribe. Meanwhile, the bulk of the raiding warriors waited 90 or more kilometres away, next to a well or source of water, so that they were undetectable by any potential victim. Once the 'explorer' returned with the desired information, they made a forced march by camel through the night, reaching their target secretively in about three or four hours. They then took positions between the dunes or rocks around the enemy in silence, rested, and attacked at the first light of dawn. The attack would take the enemy totally by surprise. Their scouts and sentries would only have patrolled the area during the day, but not at night, and certainly not to that distance.

Beyond these ambushing parties, the general movement of Arab armies could seem erratic - as the armies always advanced

Years later, and for comparison with previous picture, a group of ibn Saud's retainers preparing to dance the King of War Dance in Riyadh of the 1930s. (Popperfoto, via Almana)

in a somewhat indirect way towards their objectives. To feed and water themselves, they had to look for wells, oases, villages, pools formed by the rains, or water sources that flowed only three or four days a year. These might be found every 30 or 40 kilometres and not necessarily on a direct pathway to their objective. Thus, it was frequent that they took large detours or even appeared to retreat while on the march. As will be seen, the final struggle between the Rashidis and those of ibn Saud in 1906 consisted of a game of cat and mouse: each trying to manoeuvre to occupy the nearby wells and deprive the other of water in order to destroy his enemy by thirst and not by pitched battle.

NUMBER OF WARRIORS

Contrary to the figures described by the chroniclers, armies fighting wars in the Arabian Peninsula were never particularly sizeable – the scarcity of water alone made it impossible for large numbers of troops and animals to survive for any long time in the same place. The Rashidis, perhaps at the height of their power, at the end of the 19th century, with all the Nejd under their control, might have been able to gather 10,000 warriors, but after the loss of the central (Riyadh) and southern Nejd to the Sauds, and then the Qasim, it is likely that they did not exceed 4,000 warriors (the same as ibn Saud had in this region in 1930). Due to incessant infighting, the figure was much more often about half of that. The Hejazis of the Sharif of Mecca, likewise, are unlikely to have had more than 5,000-10,000 warriors (this was the number of troops they could pay in mid-1916, and the number of rifles they had at the end of the year), except for the moments of massive economic aid from Great Britain, late during the Great War, when this figure was tripled. In the years 1924 and 1925, Bedouin support to the Sharif was alienated by tax increases for pilgrimages to Mecca. As a result, the Hejazi army significantly decreased, perhaps to as few as 3,000 warriors, most of whom were regulars and other, non-Bedouin elements.

In front of them, the Sauds would only have about 4,000-5,000 warriors when they controlled the centre and south of the Nejd and then the Qasim, at the beginning of the century and until

Saudi armed retainers in white dresses, with their rifles, cartridge belts and long knives or swords, preparing to receive their lord. (Sander, 1939)

1908. With the conquest of al-Hasa and other regions, as part of the Hejaz and Asir, and with British aid during the Great War they may have reached 10,000 warriors in 1919, 1921 and during the Battle of Sibylla in 1929. As many, that is, as the Rashidis had at the end of the 19th Century. The creation of the Ikhwan warrior monks would bring Saud a mobilizable force of some 12,000 fanatics (from 120 convents or 'flags'). Among them, the most powerful were the Mutair, the 'Ataiba, the Ajman, the Shammar and the Harb or Harab, with a force of between 1,000 and 2,000 warriors each. The rest would have a few hundred warriors, 1,000 at most. Similarly, the citizen militias of the Nejd and Riyadh numbered around 1,500 men. Therefore, a good way to calculate Arab manpower of the time was to assign a thousand men for each tribal or city group. The largest armies mobilized by ibn Saud appeared in 1930, during the Ikhwan rebellion, when up to 16,000 tribal warriors, citizen militias and loyal Ikhwan nominally served with one army. Even then, this actually consisted of three corps: the western of the Shammari origin and made of about 4,000 former Rashidis; the centre of about 7,000-8,000 warriors under ibn Saud; and the eastern, of another 4,000 warriors from al-Hasa. Since 1929, the Sauds also had a motorised component of about 200 vehicles, including 25 armoured cars and trucks, a few mounting machine guns.

Table 1: Comparable Strength of Arab Armies, 1890s-1930

Emirate	Strength	Period
Shammar/Rashidi	10,000	1890s
Shammar/Rashidi	2,000-4,000	1903-1921
Hejaz	5,000-10,000	1916
Hejaz	26,000-30,000	1918
Hejaz	3,000	1924-1925
Kuwait	5,000	1902-1922
Riyadh/Saud	4,000-5,000	1903-1906
Nejd & Hasa/Saud	10,000	1919-1929
(Sultanate of) Nejd/Saud	16,000	1929-1930

WEAPONS

Weaponry essentially comprised of swords, knives, spears (usually made of bamboo), and above all, muzzle-loading *jazail* muskets. With the passage of time the Arabs would acquire modern weaponry, smuggled in, or supplied by the British, such as British Martini rifles, Arisaka of Japanese origin, and later, the excellent Short Magazine Lee Enfield (SMLE) calibre .303in, even Lee Enfield long rifles. Another important source of supplies was the Ottoman Empire – though usually in form of arms captured either from the Ottomans, or their Rashidi allies, such as the Ottoman-made Mauser models M1887, M1898 and M1903, the German Mauser 1898, or even the British Martini of 1904-1906. Machine guns were extremely scarce during the period covered in this volume: the few French-made Hotchkiss and British Lewis types were deployed by the enemies of the Sauds. The heavier Vickers or Maxim models were generally not used due to the need for tripods, and for water-cooling systems. Indeed, the Sauds would not acquire any before 1929, when they played a decisive role in the battle of Sibilla, which will be described in the Volume 2.

With regards to artillery: this was almost non-existent. The Saudi arsenals only had the old mountain pieces captured from the Ottomans in 1904-1908. The Hashemites, by contrast, had British and French pieces, both mountain and field, which were acquired during the First World War. The Ottomans had pieces of German and even Austrian origin. On the other hand, by 1929, the Sauds would have about twenty cars or trucks, a few protected, perhaps five, with machine guns. The Hashemites also had them, but only after the Great War. They were to prove decisive weapons in many encounters by providing the troops with incredible mobility, protection, and firepower, sometimes being able to keep at bay and disperse a party of several hundred Bedouins. Of course, the British and, to a lesser extent, the Ottomans, had plenty of these vehicles – as will be described in greater detail throughout the narrative, mainly in Volume 2. Curiously, the British armoured vehicles were considered

Captains Wood and Thorne in Bedouin dress loading a SMLE rifle. Visible in the background right is Lawrence, checking his Colt .45 automatic pistol. Taken during the Great War. (via Murphy)

Austrian mountain guns captured from the Ottomans in Tafila, in 1918, by the Hashemite Bedouins and regulars. (via IWM Q59368, via Murphy)

much too valuable to be used in combat: usually, they were held back in reserve, in case of necessity or to just protect posts and airdromes: at least in Iraq in the 1920s, mostly armed, but no armoured cars were used in larger numbers. The models were mainly Fords and Talbots as armed cars, and Rolls-Royces as armoured cars, usually armed with a Vickers machine gun or a 10-pounder gun.

With regards to aviation, this was available to the major powers – the Ottoman, the British, and the French – and to a lesser extent the Hashemites of the Hejaz during 1921-1925 (as will be seen in Volume 2). The Saudi aircraft also made their appearance during these years, though a bit later - coming too late to participate in any of the wars involving the Arabs. The main assets for war were the Bristol BE2 and F2B, the Aircos DH.9A and C, the Westland Wapitis, briefly the Short 184 and Sopwith Schneider as seaplanes, and the bizarre Vickers Victoria as bombers (all of them of British origin, with the DH.9s and Wapitis also used by the Hejazis and the Sauds). Also, the Caudrons G.6 and Breguet XIV B2 were deployed, largely by the French, as were the Pfalz A.II, Rumpler C.I and Albatross C.III by the Ottomans. To a lesser extent there was some use of Caudron G.3 and Armstrong Whitworth FK.8 by the Hejazi. These devices were primarily deployed for reconnaissance, sometimes for close air support, interdiction strikes, but also for training and liaison. No dogfights – air combats between single or multiple aircraft – occurred, but a few aircraft were destroyed by ground fire or while on the ground. Their story is going to be described in detail throughout Volume 2.[5]

British Rolls-Royce-, Ford, and Talbot armed cars in Vilayet of Syria, in 1918. Notable is the large number of replacement wheels, necessary due to the harshness of the desert terrain. (IWM Q59529, via Murphy)

THE ORIGINS OF SAUD AND WAHHABISM

Returning back to the narration of ibn Saud's 1902 feat of arms: Riyadh was the capital of the Saudi family, therefore, its conquest was of crucial importance to them. But why were the Sauds in exile? How had they come to lose their land and were now fighting to get it back? To understand, we must go back several centuries.

In the beginning, the Saudi family was originally from al-Hasa, near the coast, to the east of Riyadh. In the mid-15th Century they moved to the Nejd, in the middle of the desert, seeking the protection and help of a relative. Three centuries later, in 1726, the Sauds had acclimatized to the rigors of the land and controlled the city of Dhariya – but little else. However, in 1744 they met a 41-year-old holy man who would change their destiny: Mohammed ibn Abdul Wahhab. The man was a religious preacher whose puritanical, harsh, and fundamentalist vision of Islam was especially attractive to the hard and austere Bedouins of the desert. Forced conversion, contempt for luxury, arts, and music, and stoning for adultery were generally welcomed or at least accepted by the Sauds. Their Emir, Abdul Aziz ibn Mohammed, converted to Wahhabism and protected the preacher. Inspired by this religious doctrine and pushed to expansion by his proselytising, Abdul Aziz conquered different tribes, oases, and fields, until he entered Riyadh, the most important city of the Nejd, in 1773. Al-Hasa, the home of his ancestors, fell in 1796, and later, almost all of Oman had converted to Wahhabism. His followers continued their expansion like an oil slick and in a decentralized way, reaching, in the north, Mesopotamia - modern-day Iraqi territory – to sack Karbala in 1801. This was a holy place for the Shi'a. Contrary to the Wahhabis, who were an off-shoot of Sunni Islam, the Shi'a were the followers of the son-in-law of the Prophet Mohammed: a branch of Islam opposed to the Sunnis.

In the west, the Sauds took Taif in 1802, killing all the males, and then went on to capture Mecca that same year. The new Emir of the Sauds, the son of the previous Emir, Saud ibn Abdul Aziz 'the Great', took Medina in 1804. His followers, six years later – it remains unknown whether in their iconoclastic crusade against luxury and idolatry or for profit – looted the tomb of the Prophet Mohammed in Medina, distributing the jewels and relics deposited there. Significantly, by 1811 the Wahhabi Empire stretched from Oman to the Red Sea, and as far north as Aleppo, in Syria.

However, the destruction wrought in Medina caused a scandal in the Arab world and forced the neighbouring Ottoman Empire to act against this growing kingdom which threatened its supremacy over the Sunni world. Thus, the Pasha of Egypt, Mohammed Ali, took Medina and Mecca in 1812 and 1813. The two holy cities would remain in Ottoman hands until the end of First World War, just as the Ottoman Sultan – always a member of the Ottoman Dynasty (House of Osman) - remained the Caliph, the religious leader of the Sunni world. This lasted until the creator of modern-day Turkey/Türkiye, Kemal Pasha Atatürk, abolished the caliphate on 1 November 1922, leaving one of biggest religions of the World leaderless to this very day.

In 1818-1819, an Ottoman counteroffensive drove into the interior of the Nejd, and razed Dhariya to its foundations. Saud the Great's son, Emir Abdullah, in an incredible gesture of courage and generosity, agreed to surrender to the Ottomans and be beheaded in exchange for the life of his family. Thus, although the Sauds lost their empire and became a second-rate force, thanks to Abdullah's sacrifice, they continued to exist to fight another day. By 1824, a side branch of the Saudis, under the Amir Turki, regained the pre-eminence of the Sauds in the Nejd, although they were now isolated in the middle of the desert. The Ottomans returned in 1836 to contain this expansion. Nevertheless, Turki's son Faisal the Great, after escaping from an Egyptian prison, managed to recover the Saud territories of central Arabia to their extent of 1800 – except for Oman and Yemen, and, of course, without controlling the Holy Places of Islam. One of his main allies was a feudatory Abdullah ibn Rashid: he grew strong enough to achieve independence, and controlled the area of the mountains of Shammar or Jebel Shammar, in the north of the Nejd, from his capital, Häil. The Rashidis, in fact, would become ibn Saud's greatest rivals for control of the Nejd, and they fought him bitterly until their defeat in 1921.

Mohammed ibn Abdullah ar-Rashid, called Rashid The Great, conquered all Nejd and forced the Sauds to become his subjects. (The Book of Tuhfat al-Mushtaq fi Akhbar Najd, Hijaz, and Iraq)

On the death of Faisal the Great in 1865, the Sauds entered a period of civil war. The Ottomans exploited this situation to return in 1871, via the water – the Persian Gulf – to al-Hasa, taking Hofuf, and depriving the Sauds of their access to the sea. This territory would remain in Ottoman hands until 1913. That's when the father of The Leopard, Abdur Rahman (another son of Faisal the Great), appeared on the scene. Liberated by the Ottomans, the patriarch left Iraq for al-Hasa, leading an anti-Ottoman uprising in 1874. The revolt failed, but Abdur Rahman took refuge in Riyadh, where one of his brothers reigned. The civil war continued between the brothers, until they all gathered in 1876 to agree on an order of succession (Abdur Rahman would be the last to reign, in 1899) and to expel another of the brothers, whose children would become the Araif, the cousins and another of the enemies of ibn Saud. In fact, it was on this date of the peace accord that our protagonist, ibn Saud, was born, on 15 January 1876.

With the end of the quarrels between the brothers, the Sauds tried for several years to subdue their former Rashidi subjects, without success. Their efforts were interrupted again when the Araifs, the sons of the exiled brother, managed to seize power in Riyadh in 1888. At the same time, the Rashidis also had a succession crisis that Mohammed ibn Abdullah ar-Rashid, known as 'The Great', solved with a massacre of his relatives. Rashid the Great, seeing that his Saudi rivals were troubled by their succession chaos, exploited the opportunity to attack Riyadh and expel the Araif, placing Abdur Rahman's brothers in power once again. In fact, for all practical purposes, the Sauds became a protectorate of the Rashidi; the Rashidi even appointed a governor. In 1890 the governor announced that he wanted to visit ibn Saud's father, Emir Abdur Rahman. But, fearing that the governor would assassinate him, Saud's father pre-empting any ambush went ahead and attacked. After killing all the bodyguards, he successfully captured the governor. Rashid the Great reacted by besieging Riyadh for 40 days, that was until the people begged Abdur Rahman to surrender to avoid further suffering. Rashid was generous, and ibn Saud's father had to leave Riyadh, but was appointed governor of Aridh, in the centre of the Nedj.

Abdur Rahman saw his chance again when excessive taxes levied by Rashid the Great on the fertile area of Qasim put the province in rebellion in 1891. However, the Rashidis were quicker and crushed the revolt before ibn Saud's father arrived. What was worse, having had his plot discovered, he had to leave his lands and go into exile to avoid being beheaded. After a long journey, ibn Saud's family ended up in the terrible Rub'al-Khali, the most inhospitable area of all the deserts of Arabia, inhabited only by the Murra. Here, ibn Saud, barely a teenager, would learn with the toughest to survive in the harshest of deserts. After a number of failed attempts by Abdur Rahman to retake Riyadh, he and his family finally received a small subsidy from the Ottomans. In 1896, they became refugees in Kuwait, at the Court of Sheikh Mubarak as Sabah. Mubarak would become a friend and mentor to ibn Saud, teaching him the first rudiments of trade, diplomacy and international relations in a territory that flirted with both the Ottomans and the British. There, ibn Saud had his first contacts with British officers, as Kuwait, in 1899, would become a British Protectorate.

After the death of Rashid the Great in 1897, Abdur Rahman again decided to try to recover his territories and formed an alliance with Sheikh Mubarak of Kuwait to defeat the Rashidis. By early 1901, the Sauds managed to concentrate some 5,000 warriors from the Ajman, Suhul, Mutair, Murra, and Muntafiq Bedouins of southern Iraq. It should be kept in mind that Kuwait was larger at that time than it is today and most of these tribes belonged to the jurisdiction of

Abdur Rahman or Abd el-Rahman, father of ibn Saud, attempted to recover the Saudi lands from the Rashidis, failing several times, but ably delegated power to his son ibn Saud when he took Riyadh. (Historical Atlas of Saudi Arabia, Darat Al-Malik Abdulaziz)

Kuwait's Mubarak. On 18 March, this army confronted the new Emir of Shammar, Abdul Aziz ibn Mitab ar Rashid, at Tarafiya, 25km east of Buraida, in the central Nejd, in the Qasim area. Ar-Rashid proved to be a bad politician, but as effective military commander as Rashid the Great: he destroyed the allied army. Then he appeared in front of the walls of Kuwait City. Only the British fleet and the militias in the city prevented ibn Rashid from overrunning the place. At the same time, his troops committed a massacre in Buraida, for supporting the Sauds. The Leopard was not present at that time in the battle, but in command of a small party swarming around Riyadh, analysing its weak points. Their group grew with the arrival of the Ajman, al-Murra, Subai and even Suhul from southern Arabia, eventually growing to several thousand warriors: only the Ottoman declaration of support for the Rashidi caused them to dissolve. The following year, 1902, ibn Saud would then manage to take Riyadh by surprise, as described in the introduction, thus starting the fire that would light up the entire Middle East and all of the Muslim world.[6]

2

FIRST SAUDI RASHIDI WAR, 1902–1909

Once ibn Saud had recovered Riyadh, a large number of Bedouin sheikhs in southern Nejd confirmed their support for him. Soon after, in May 1902, the Saud family, with their Patriarch Abdur Rahman, left their exile in Kuwait to settle in their ancestral capital. At the same time, Abdur Rahman gave ibn Saud, only 26 years old, a ceremonial sword with its scabbard coated in silver and gold. He also granted his son the title of Emir, although he kept for himself the title of Imam, or religious leader. Meanwhile, Riyadh's crumbling defences were rebuilt, in preparation for a counterattack from the Rashidi – which never materialised. Ibn Saud went south to visit the tribes that had never before submitted to ibn Rashid, and secured an alliance of the Hariq, in the Kharj; of the austere Murra, in the great desert of Rub' al-Khali (his former allies and the first place of Saudi refuge); and the tribes in the districts of Hauta and Aflaj. The alliance grew but nevertheless, the Ajmans, located in the northeast, towards the coast, and protected by the presence of Ottoman forces in the area, refused to join.

THE RASHIDI REACTION: THE BATTLE OF DILAM

Finally, sometime in late July or early August 1902, the army of Abdul Aziz ibn Mitaab ar-Rashid – son of Rashid the Great, therefore known as ibn Rashid, the 6th Emir of Jebel Shammar – set out against Riyadh. First, he subdued the lands of Washm, Mhamal and Qasim, who were in revolt. Ibn Rashid's fame for courage was legendary, his diplomatic skills or as an administrator – not so much. This mattered not: he was the stuff of legend. One instance of this was at a meeting with several feudatory tribal chiefs: here, a small desert scorpion got between the layers of his clothes and began to sting him repeatedly. The sting of a desert scorpion is not deadly, but it is tremendously painful. Even so, ibn Rashid remained with his guests for several hours, absorbing the pain without complaint, until he could get rid of the animal once they had all left.

To stop ibn Rashid, Abdur Rahman, Saud's father, was left defending Riyadh with 1,000 warriors, while Sa´ad, one of his sons, raised a force in Hariq. Ibn Saud himself marched to the south to recruit another body among the citizen militias of Aridh, Hauta, and Duwasir, as well as in the al-Murra and Shamir tribes. Then, ibn Saud, though inferior in numbers, followed ibn Rashid, dodging combat and cutting off his enemy´s water sources during September and October. At last, this water shortage caused an epidemic that weakened the Rashidi forces. Still, ibn Rashid arrived at Riyadh with 4,000 men in October, only to see that he could not take it, and with the risk to be trapped between the garrison of Abdur Rahman and the force of ibn Saud outside. He opted, therefore, to cut off Saud's supply lines with Kuwait, and, at the same time, to attack the southern provinces that joined the Sauds. Ibn Rashid moved his army to Dilam, about 80km southeast of Riyadh, intending to take it before the arrival of Saud. He arrived at dusk, camping outside the city. Ibn Saud would arrive during the night with 2,000 warriors, reinforcing the garrison. At dawn on January 27, 1903, the Rashidi cavalry advanced against the Sauds, but the Sauds had entrenched themselves between the walls and palm trees on the outskirts of the town, and disorganised the attackers by heavy rifle fire. Then the Saudi cavalry counterattacked, leaving ibn Rashid without a choice

Ibn Saud´s clan during a meeting in Kuwait in 1911. In the first row, from left to right, ibn Saud, then the Sheikh Mubaraq of Kuwait, and then Mohammed, half brother of ibn Saud. Behind them, in the second row, between Saud and Mubaraq, visible is Sa´ad, other brother of The Leopard. (Royal Geographic Society, via Almana)

but to order a retreat to Hafar al-Atj, 140km north-east of Riyadh. The Rashidi were not to know that the Sauds had exhausted almost all their ammunition.

Table 2: Battle of Dilam, 27 January 1903

Emirate	Allied Tribes	Strength	Notes
Shammar/Rashidi		4,000	led by ibn Rashid
Nejd/Saud		2,500	led by ibn Saud
	Hariq levies		led by Sa'ad
	Aridh levies		
	Hauta levies		
	Duwasir levies		
	Dilam garrison	perhaps 500	
	al-Murra Bedouin		
	Shamir Bedouin		

Abdul Aziz ibn Mitab ar Rashid, son of Rashid the Great, known as ibn Rashid, 6th Amir of Jebel (or the Mountain) Shammar, brave and a talented military leader, ended killed by ibn Saud in 1906. Harsh and hot-tempered he alienated the favour of his Qasim subjects, and killed his own Ottoman commanding officer in a discussion. (Shmmer)

In January 1903, seeing that the British, through their delegation in Bahrain, were going to remain neutral, the Sauds signed an alliance against the Rashidis with Kuwait and the Muntafiq tribe of Mesopotamia, under Sadoon. As if eager to worsen his position, in February 1903, the cunning ibn Rashid threatened to attack Kuwait. In turn, the local Sheikh of Kuwait played both sides, writing to ibn Rashid at the same time as he did to the Sauds. On one occasion Mubarak's secretary mistook the letters and sent those addressed to ibn Rashid to ibn Saud, and vice versa, which caused ibn Saud to laugh at the wiles of his old Kuwaiti master and friend. Ibn Saud departed with a relief force containing tribal contingents from the Ajman, al-Murra, Subai, Suhul, Bani Hajir, Bani Khalid, and Awazim, and together with another Kuwaiti force under Jabir, son of the Kuwait Sheikh. In all, they numbered about 10,000 warriors and 500 horsemen. This huge Saudi-Kuwaiti force plundered the Mutair region, an allied tribe of the Rashidis, halfway between Kuwait and Riyadh, killing their leader Ammash ad-Duwish. Ibn Rashid did not fall into this trap, however, and took advantage of the absence of these forces to fall like lightning on the defenceless Riyadh. The surprise was spoiled only because the Suhul tribe observed the arrival of ibn Rashid and warned the citizens of Riyadh, who were able to prepare for defence. After a series of skirmishes on 3 and 4 April, seeing the city well defended, ibn Rashid retreated to the north. Abdul Rahman took the opportunity to venture out of Riyadh to follow him and take Shaqra, 120km to the

Ibn Saud's Army with his flags deployed, ready to charge, during exercises in the Thaj area in 1911. Picture taken by Captain Shakespear. (Royal Geographic Society, Shakespear 1911, via *Desperta Ferro*)

Prince Sa´ad, younger brother of ibn Saud, who led the Hariq tribes in 1902-1903, extracted from a family picture taken in Kuwait in 1911. (Royal Geographic Society, Shakespear 1911, via Sander)

Sheikh Mubaraq of Kuwait, friend of the Saud family, and teacher of ibn Saud in political tricks and relations with the Western countries. (Royal Geographic Society, Shakespear 1911, via Sander)

northwest. Soon, ibn Saud joined his father, who with his forces took Majma and Zilfi. Then, ibn Rashid marched to Qasim in May and erected a fort at Tharmida, in the Washm region, to protect his domains from an attack from this direction. Furthermore, he reinforced the garrisons of his main cities in the Qasim region, Buraida and Anaiza.[1]

THE SAUDI COUNTERATTACK

Ibn Saud launched his counteroffensive in the summer, and precisely where ibn Rashid had anticipated, through Tharmida in Washm, south of Qasim and southwest of Riyadh. In April, ibn Saud's cousin, ibn Jiluwi of the Riyadh deed, took the place, massacring the Rashidi garrison after two months of siege. Then, the Saudi army moved towards Sudair, surrounding Qasim to the east. Emir Rashidi was not very popular among the population, and the prestige of ibn Saud was huge after the victory of Dilam and the taking of Tharmida. Unsurprisingly, many villages of Washm, Sudair and Qasim – such as Shaqra, Tahdiq, Ghat, Jalajil, and Raudhat as Sudair – opened their doors to the Sauds. By the winter of 1903, The Leopard thus controlled most of fertile Arabia, the central and southern Nejd. Upon his return, a meeting of Ulema in Riyadh proclaimed ibn Saud an Emir and Imam of the Wahhabis.

The Mismak Fort, in Riyadh, as seen from the Royal Palace. (Philby, 1928, via Sander)

In 1904, ibn Rashid departed to Mesopotamia to recruit reinforcements and aid from the Ottoman sanjaks in the *Vilayet* (Province) Baghdad. Taking advantage of his absence, and after the first rains left good pastures, ibn Saud set out in a north-western direction, to subdue the two main Rashidi cities of Qasim – Anaiza (or Unayzah) and Buraida - which controlled the caravan route from Kuwait to Mecca. At the beginning of March, ibn Saud destroyed a Rashidi force in Raudhat as-Sirr, 75km west of Shaqra, because this was preventing him from passing to Anaiza. At dawn on the 22nd, ibn Saud launched an assault on Anaiza itself with a group of natives of this city who had joined him, as well as 100 warriors from Riyadh led by his cousin ibn Jiluwi. Anaiza was taken, and the Rashidi local commander Majid ibn Hamud was killed in cavalry combat. Immediately after, ibn Saud turned around and with his cavalry destroyed another force of horsemen of the Araif, the rival Saudi branch in the service of the Rashidis, in Wadi ar-Rumah as this attempted to reach Anaiza. After the defeat, part of this contingent was integrated into the Saudi forces. According to ibn Saud, in this battle 370 Rashidis fell in exchange for only two of his men.

Considering the Rashidi Emirate was as powerful as that of the Sauds, it´s surprising that his reaction was rather lukewarm. Perhaps it was due to the number of casualties suffered. Perhaps it was also due to the claim that the Rashidi rule was very harsh, cruel and that it imposed excessive taxes. This appeared likely to hold some truth, because the cities and tribes began switching to ibn Saud almost without resistance – at least in Qasim and Washm, in the centre of the Nejd. As his governor of Anaiza, ibn Saud appointed Abd al-Aziz al-Sulaim.

Sometime in early June, during evening prayer, a group of Saud sympathizers, the al-Muhanna, opened the gates of Buraida, just 22km north of Anaiza. The 150 men of the Rashidi garrison had to flee into the citadel. After ten weeks of blockade, a force of Rashidis under Ubadi ar-Rashid came to their aid, but ibn Saud defeated them. As Ubaid had murdered an uncle of ibn Saud ten years earlier, when The Leopard saw him, he plunged his sword into his belly and stirred it until his guts were exposed. Until then, ibn Saud still enforced the Law of Talion as harshly as his enemies. Subsequently, he would become wiser and tolerant, and shrewdly turned into a compassionate leader practicing forgiveness: this was to earn him a huge number of grateful supporters. To finally resolve the siege at Buraida, the Sauds made a tunnel under the citadel wall and blew it up, forcing the surrender of the city: the garrison was permitted to evacuate with weapons and baggage, and the city was then entrusted to the al-Muhanna, rivals of the Rashidi in the region.[2]

OTTOMAN GUNS AGAINST ARAB SPEARS: BATTLE OF BUKAIRIYA

We left ibn Rashid appealing for help from the Ottoman Empire. He could do so because, actually, he was a subject of the Sultan in Constantinople. In this appeal, he contacted the Wali or governor of the *Vilayet* Baghdad. At the time, the Ottomans were already busy constructing a railway line from Damascus to Medina, and the last thing they wanted was a Nejd in flames. Therefore, they decided to support ibn Rashid, and sent him money and weapons. With this equipment he could recruit the tribes of the Harb and Hutaim. The two tribes lived on a long strip of land between Qasim and Shammar. This tribal district was very extensive, reaching in its western area the Red Sea, Medina and Mecca, but it is unlikely that the Rashidi allies from this area could muster more than 2,000 warriors. The Hutaim were further north, but in a strip parallel to the coastal area of the Hejaz in a north-south direction (without reaching the sea), close to the border of present-day Jordan. These troops were joined by their own Shammari contingents, along with citizen militias from their capital, Häil. Due to the fact the first contemporary contact with the Ottomans was at the beginning of the year, it remains unknown if these were the forces that fought against ibn Saud until June, or whether they were formed later.

In addition to these tribal levies, at the end of May of 1904 the first regular Ottoman Army units arrived in Häil from Samara (or Samawa) on the Euphrates. These were 2,000 or 2,400 men organized into four reduced regiments. The Ottoman Army garrisoning the Vilayet Baghdad was still in the process of being built-up, and it is probable that its first division established in this area – either the 11th or the 12th – also had this quadrangular organisation: that it consisted of four regiments with a total of, perhaps, more than six battalions (probably 8-11), along with a battery of six mule-towed artillery pieces.[3] Each of Ottoman troops arrived together with 800 rounds of Martini ammunition, and the entire force was commanded by Colonel Hassan Shukri.

The city of Anaiza, or Unayzah, one of the two main cities of the Qasim, taken by ibn Saud in March 1904. (Popperfoto, via Almana)

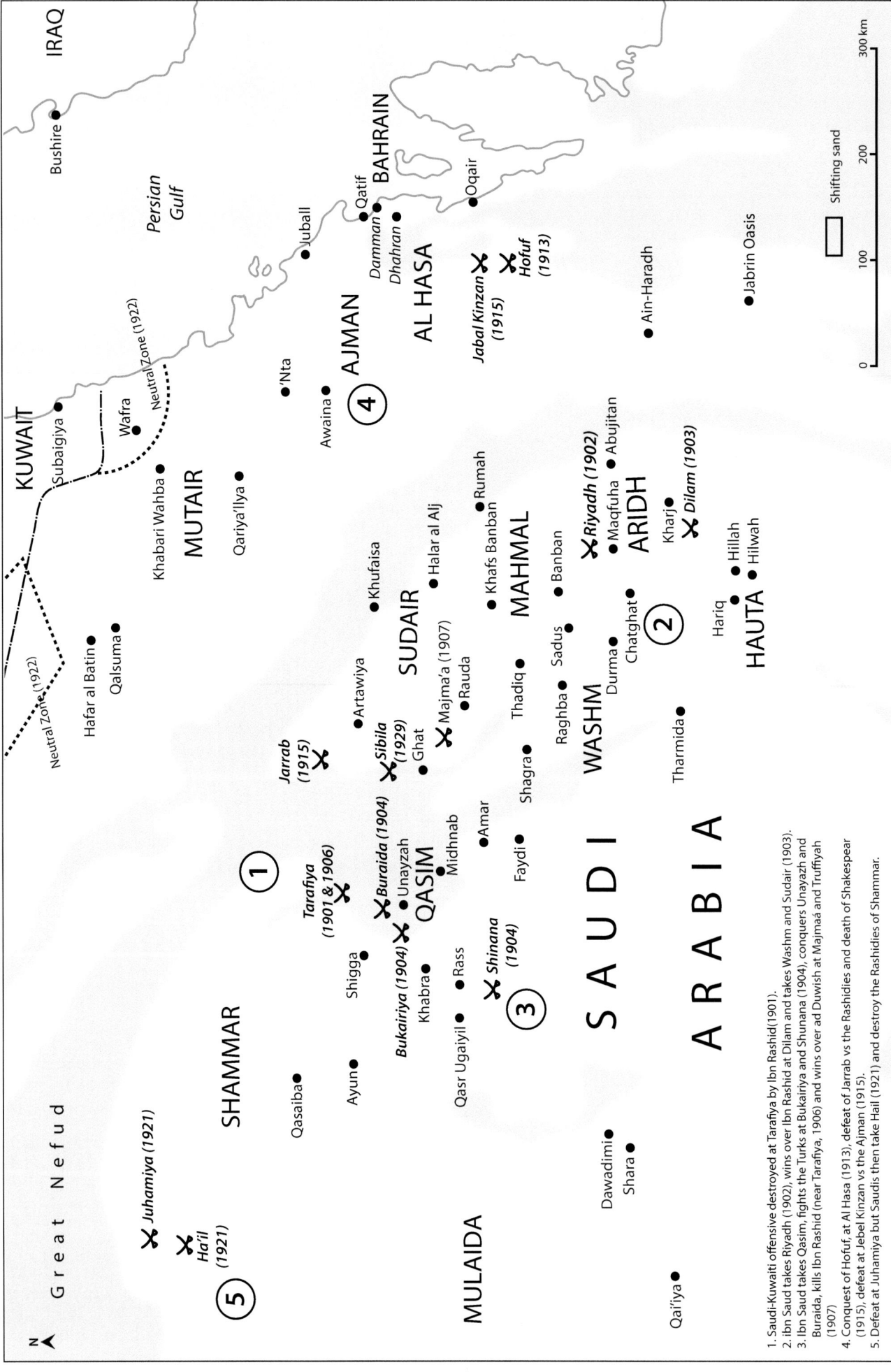

Main battles and actions in central Nejd. (Map by George Anderson based on Sander and de Gabiola)

Ibn Saud reacted by requesting help from the then 'British resident in the Persian Gulf', Major Cox, 'warning' him that the Ottomans were about to conquer the entire area. There was no reaction. Certain the Ottoman artillery could easily tear down the clay brick walls of Buraida, ibn Saud left the village and marched to Bukairiya, an area cleared of sand and with some palm trees, 30km west of Anaiza, where his cavalry could manoeuvre. In principle, he expected to count on the militias of Riyadh, the tribes of al-Khar (especially the al-Murra), and part of the Mutair, former Rashidis. These were about 3,000 warriors. However, the urban militias of the newly conquered Qasim and part of the Mutair, under ibn Jiluwi, perhaps another 2,000 men, had not yet arrived.

Table 3: Battle of Bukairiya, 15 July 1904

Emirate	Allied Forces	Strength	Notes
Shammar/Rashidi		2,000	led by ibn Rashidi
Ottoman Army		2,200-2,5,000, 6 guns	Colonel Shukri; probably including elements from 11th and/ or 12th Divisions
Nejd/Saud		3,000	led by ibn Saud
	Riyadh Militia		
	al-Murra Bedouin		
	Mutair Bedouin		former Rashidi
Nejd/Saud Relief Force		2,000	led by Ibn Jiluwi, arriving at the end of battle
	Qasim Militia		
	Mutair Bedouin		

The battle was joined at dawn on 15 July 1904. The Bedouin cavalry from the south of the Nejd and the urban militias under ibn Saud, charged the Rashidi horsemen, numbering perhaps 2,000, and scattered them, only to find that farther behind, the Ottoman Army troops had formed a square, with their bayonets up and cannons situated in the corners. The Sauds were quickly destroyed by their fire: essentially, ibn Rashidi and Shukri had lured ibn Saud into a trap, forcing him to attack with a feigned flight, aiming to draw them onto the Ottoman firepower. A cannon shell landed near ibn Saud himself, shrapnel injuring his hand and knee. The Leopard had to retreat to receive medical attention, and by the time he returned his force had been decimated by the enemy firepower. Left without a choice, ibn Saud retreated about 75 kilometres to the southeast, to Midhnab. It was at that time that the Saudi militias from the towns of Qasim, along with Mutair's troops under Saud's cousin, ibn Jiluwi, arrived at the empty battlefield to attack the enemies that had dispersed to loot the Saudi camp. Depending on the source, either this last-minute attack saved part of the day for the Sauds, or it was quickly dispersed by the Ottomans. Whichever was the case, the Sauds had been defeated. Their claims to have killed 1,500 Ottomans and 500 Rashidis, are rather incredible, as that would represent about half of their opponents. Actually, the Rashidi chronicles recorded about 100 dead of the Shammaris, and 200 of the Sauds. When one adds the wounded to the calculation, this is almost certainly closer to the correct figures for casualties.[4]

A PYRRHIC VICTORY: SHUNANA

Following the victory, Colonel Hassan Shukri split his and Rashidi forces into several groups and advanced to recapture some of the cities of Qasim. Undeterred, ibn Saud took the opportunity to launch a nightime counterattack against the camp of a Rashidi

Ottoman soldier wearing a red Fez cap with blue tassel and his dark blue uniform, pattern M1893. He wears thick woollen leggings tucked into socks, and a pair of peasant shoes. Notable is his M1890 Mauser carbine and four bandoliers for ammunition. This picture was taken in 1912, before the Balkans War, but the soldier, being a Rediff, a reservist, is wearing the old uniform worn during the operations of 1904. (Dr David Nicolle Collection)

force besieging Khabra, taking part of its supplies. Meanwhile, the main body of ibn Rashid and Shukri's troops attacked ar-Rass, southwest of Anaiza, which had revolted. This forced Saud's brother Mohammed to leave the walls of the city. During this time, ibn Saud returned to his lands to gather reinforcements from the Mutair, located east and west of Qasim, and from the ´Ataiba or Utaibah, to the west, between Riyadh and Mecca. Then he returned to the area of Qasim in the middle of August. He encamped his force in Shinana or Shunana, 18km southwest of ar-Rass, to help the rebels. The Rashidis and Ottomans were actually waiting for them in this place, but their ranks were greatly weakened by an outbreak of cholera. For two months the opponents skirmished, indicating both their numerical parity, and lack of interest in risking battle. However, when both sides began suffering their first desertions, major combat became only a matter of time. Frustrated, ibn Rashid retreated to the northwest, followed by ibn Saud. The Leopard, recognizing signs of weakness amongst his enemies, decided to give pursuit and then attack.

The fierce Prince Mohammed, the half-brother of ibn Saud, who was in the rear-guard during the capture of Riyadh in 1902, and had a prominent part in the victory of Shunana, as seen in a photo taken in 1911 in Kuwait. Brave and hot-tempered, he quarrelled with the Prince of Kuwait ending an old alliance between these two Emirates. (Photo by Shakespear 1911, via Sander)

On 27 September 1904, ibn Saud sent a small force led by his brother Mohammed to block the Rashidi route. They achieved this by taking and defending the oasis of Qasr ibn'Uqaiyil. The Ottomans attacked but, after a few hours, realised they could not dislodge the enemy in front of them, whilst, all the while, ibn Saud was approaching from behind. They collected their cannons and turned north, continuing their withdrawal under the cover of the Rashidi cavalry. Early on 28 September, they reached Wadi ar-Rumah. What happened next is difficult to figure out because the information is contradictory. Apparently, the Rashidis wanted to save the loot from their campaign and sent a part of their force north with the convoy. However, the Saudi scouts detected this move and dispatched some of their cavalry and camel-mounted warriors to pursue, while the Saudi infantry and remaining horsemen followed in the wake. Eventually, all the Rashidi booty was captured by ibn Saud near al-Bukairiya, greatly angering ibn Rashid, who reacted in terrible and irrational fashion.

The main Ottoman-Rashidi force had remained deployed further south, in a defensive position along the dry course of the Rumah River, with the Ottoman Army and its cannons in the centre, flanked by Rashidi cavalry. Ibn Rashid apparently argued with Colonel Shukri, because the Ottomans did not want to attack the Sauds, or perhaps this reluctance was a result of their retreat the day before. In the middle of the argument, ibn Rashid shot Shukri in the head and killed him. This provoked a fire-fight, during which, according to the Rashidis, more than 190 Ottomans were killed. The Leopard was quick to exploit the situation: realising the enemy ranks were reeling amid infighting, ibn Saud unleashed his cavalry. The Ottomans and Rashidis resisted bitterly, nevertheless, almost causing a collapse of his right flank, but ibn Saud then led his best horsemen into an assault on the centre. Facing attack from all sides, the Ottoman square broke and then the Rashidis fled the battlefield. As a consequence, some 550 Ottoman Army troops were killed, and they lost all of their six guns: only some 700 managed to flee the battlefield. Despite their triumph, the Sauds themselves probably suffered up to 500 casualties. Collecting all the loot from the battlefield, they withdrew from Anazia for Riyadh on 12 October 1905.

The extent to which ibn Saud was shaken by his pyrrhic victory, and by how much he was still dependent on Ottoman subsidies (which he was still receiving from Constantinople, just like the Rashidis were), is confirmed by a letter to the Sultan in Constantinople, which he wrote immediately after the battle. In this, he stressed he still recognised the Sultan as his lord, and requested forgiveness for having attacked his troops.[5]

Table 4: ibn Saud's Forces during the Battle of Shunana, 27-28 September 1904

Emirate	Allied Forces	Strength	Notes
Nejd/Saud		Around 5,000	ibn Saud & Mohammed
	Mutair Bedouin		
	'Ataiba Bedouin		
	al-Murra Bedouin		
	Qasim Militia		
	Riyadh Militia		

QASIM AS A BUFFER STATE

In January 1905, the Ottomans deployed a relief force of 3,000 soldiers and another battery of six cannons under Ahmad Faizi Pasha from Najaf, in Iraq, in a southern direction. At the same time, another column of 750 troops and another battery under Sidki Pasha – probably drawn from the 16th Division – left Medina, aiming to join the first column. By 15 April 1905, after collecting the survivors of the Battle of Shunana, they had a force of 4,500 troops and 12 guns, commanded by Colonel Faizi Pasha, at Buraida, in the Qasim.

In February, before pushing farther south – and also because of an armed revolt in Yemen, which had launched its war of independence under Imam Yahya (Faizi Pasha was appointed the commander of that expedition, whereupon Sidki Pasha took over in Qasim) – the Ottomans attempted to negotiate. Respectfully, they accepted a visit by a delegation led by Abdur Rahman, father of ibn Saud, to Mesopotamia. Negotiations resulted in an agreement whereby the Sauds would retain southern Nejd, with the Ottoman title of district governor (*Qaimaqam*), while the area of Qasim would be turned into a neutral buffer state between them and the Rashidi, protected by Ottoman garrisons in Buraida and Anaiza.

As a demonstration of their good faith, the Sauds left the area. They took the opportunity to march to the coast of the Persian Gulf and appease their tribal subjects of al-Hasa, the Murra, Beni Hajar and Ajman, who were fighting each other, east and southeast of Riyadh. When ibn Saud made moves in direction of Abu Dhabi and Oman, a British warning prevented him from continuing in that direction. In turn, the son of the Sheikh of Qatar – who had taken advantage of the situation to attack his brother with support of the Murra – was forced to flee to Bahrain.

Meanwhile, in Qasim, infighting erupted between the al-Muhanna, who had been left under the tutelage of the Ottomans. Despite ibn Saud's (apparent) agreement of the abandonment of the Qasim region, he played a game of double-cross, and deployed Bedouin forces under his brother Mohammed to attack several Ottoman supply convoys. In early 1906, after returning to Riyadh,

Ottoman troops inaugurating the Damascus-Medina railway in 1908. Notable are the Fez and blue uniforms, as worn during the campaigns of 1904-1906. (Mesut Uyar)

ibn Saud planned an expedition to Qasim, led by himself and including his Bedouins, the citizen militia and reinforcements from Salih al-Muhanna of Buraida. At that point in time, however, he discovered correspondence between his friend Mubarak, the Emir of Kuwait, and al-Muhanna, urging him to ally with the Rashidi. In these inhospitable lands, it was common to use duplicity for survival.

As for the Kuwaitis, Saud played dumb, but he did react by sending home the Muhanna contingent from Buraida. Still there was a strong contingent of the Mutair, north of Riyadh. At this time, the tribe was led by Faisal al-Duwaish. For nearly two decades, al-Duwaish was one of Saud's primary allies. Only much later on would he betray him and become a bitter enemy: one that not only almost provoked a war with the British Empire, but did cause a 'civil' war that will be described in Volume 2.[6]

THE DEATH OF IBN RASHID

As Saud reached Makhma'a, a place between Buraida and Riyadh, he heard that ibn Rashid had set out with 2,500 cavalry and was plundering the eastern desert, but with a smaller force than he usually had with him. Ibn Saud set out in search of Rashid. Both sides seemed to be similar in numbers, so instead of trying to attack, they dodged each other for three months; one trying to occupy the other's water wells to gain some advantage, and vice versa. At one point, ibn Rashid outflanked ibn Saud in his manoeuvres, and in a lightning march eastward crossed the escarpment of Al-Qasim just southeast of Unaiza or Unayzah, to the rear of ibn Saud, cutting off his supplies from Riyadh. With this, a part of the Saudi army was disbanded, and The Leopard was left with only 200 warriors. Saud was lost unless he struck a bold blow.

On 13 April the Sauds saw an opportunity to surprise the Rashidis in their camp at Raudhat al-Muhanna, a depression where rainwater accumulates (*raudhat*), 30km northeast of Buraida. Before dawn that day, they advanced on foot, in silence (avoiding the noise of galloping horses), until only a dune separated them from their enemy. Fortunately for them, the Rashidis had been divided into several smaller camps for logistic reasons, so the disadvantage in the number of the Sauds was less than it seemed. But, because his situation was actually desperate, due to the great numerical inferiority, ibn Saud was persuaded to stay to the rear, which he – reluctantly – accepted to do. He initiated the assault by splitting his force into two groups that, at dawn, attacked the main enemy camp from two opposite directions. This created the impression the Rashidis were surrounded. According to some sources, the attack occurred in the middle of a sandstorm and the versions differ about what subsequently happened. It seems that the attack was intended to reach the tent of ibn Rashid and to kill him without making a sound. When the attackers were already infiltrated deep within the enemy camp, a Saudi standard-bearer dropped their flag. At this rattling noise, ibn Rashid woke up and came out of his tent addressing this standard-bearer al-Fraikh - as that was the name of ibn Rashid's personal standard-bearer. The Amir had been discovered. '*This is the man!*' shouted those of ibn Saud. When ibn Rashid approached the banner, he discovered with horror that it was that of the Sauds. The standard bearer fired five shots at Rashid killing him instantly. Another, less romantic version, cites ibn Rashid rushing to the fight to encourage his followers, mistakingly taking the Saudi standard as his own, before being recognised and killed on the spot. The rest of the fighting was chaotic. The Rashidis fled when their leader fell, thinking they were surrounded. Thus, and so randomly, and with the loss of only 35 Saudi warriors, the great enemy of the Sauds, ibn Rashid fell. His head, once cut off, was taken to Buraida as an example, where it was thrown to the dogs. After this debacle, the Rashidi Emirate of Shammar would descend into a deep crisis that would last for years, until 1921; its successive leaders indulging in infighting and murdering one another, despite all being relatives.[7]

THE FINAL CONQUEST OF QASIM

Ibn Saud then considered taking advantage of the situation and marching against Häil, where different family branches of the Rashidis were already engaged in a dispute for power. However, the Ottoman subsidy to the Rahsidis was still greater than that of the Sauds (200 GBP per month versus 90 GBP). This was a clear indication of Constantinople's preference for ibn Saud's enemies. He was forced, therefore, to be careful. In addition, the route to Häil,

600km from Riyadh, was cut by the Qasim region protected by the Ottomans, and controlled by the al-Muhanna, who could not be trusted. It was now ibn Saud decided to finish them off.

In May 1906, he arrested Salih al-Muhanna and locked him up. At the same time, ibn Saud increased the pressure upon the Ottoman garrison of Qasim (probably elements of the 16th Division), and in June of the same year prohibited all tribes under his control to communicate with or provide supplies to them. With their besieged troops facing starvation and defections, in August 1906, the Ottoman Army deployed a battalion of 500-600 troops from Medina. Led by Sami Pasha al-Faruki, this entered the desert of Arabia – now notorious amongst Ottoman troops for its harshness, and renowned as 'the daughter of Satan' – and both managed not only to re-open the supply link, but also to reach and reinforce the garrison in Qasim. However, once there, Faruki promptly figured out that the situation was untenable. He entered negotiations with ibn Saud, aiming to save face while at least formally maintaining the situation in the interest of the Sultan in Constantinople. Ibn Saud feigned anger in an attempt to intimidate, shouting at Faruki that only the fact he was his guest prevented him from killing the Ottoman on the spot. Left without a choice, the Ottomans left Qasim. They left behind a symbolic force of about two dozen, who were to act as representatives of the Sultan, but without the right to intervene in local affairs or meddle into the administration of the district. On 3 November 1906, 1,200 troops and 12 guns left for Medina, while in mid-December the balance of the unit marched in direction of Basra. The tiny Ottoman garrison of Qasim survived until 1908: for all practical purposes, the Sauds now controlled the centre and the south of the Nejd – and this with the consent of the Sultan.

Further north, chaos among the Rashidis continued, as on 29 December 1906, the new Emir of Shammar, Mitab ibn Abdul Aziz, was assassinated. As was to be expected, this promptly encouraged ibn Saud to launch an opportunistic – and completely improvised – expedition against Häil. The operation did not reach its objective as the Mutair of al-Duwaish, to the east of Qasim, fearing the Saudis were growing too powerful, sided with the Rashidis. Indeed, al-Duwaish then fomented a rebellion in May 1907 by the governor of Buraida, Abd al-Khayl, and another in Muhanna – and that by a faction at least theoretically more inclined towards the Saudis. However, The Leopard entered Buraida with an army formed mainly by the 'Ataiba, subduing the rebels, and then intercepting the Mutair of al-Duwaish at Makhma'a, in the southeast, halfway between Buraida and Riyadh. Al-Duwaish was defeated and seriously wounded, but ibn Saud quickly realised that his earlier harshness would only lead to another vicious circle. To the astonishment of almost everybody, he pardoned al-Duwaish.[8]

THE BATTLE OF TRUFFIYAH AND THE SECOND PARDON OF AL-DUWAISH

At that point, The Leopard turned his attention on the Rashidi army led by a new Emir, Sultan ibn Hamud, that had arrived too late to aid the rebels. This included elements of Shammar (Buraida of Aba al-Khail), and a part of Mutair under al-Duwaish – who had rebelled again, despite ibn Saud's pardon. In battle that erupted on 22 September 12 kilometres north of Anaiza, it was promptly destroyed by the Saudi army, including citizen levies from al-Arid and Bedouins of the Qahtan, 'Ataiba, Subai and Suhul tribes. Ironically, ibn Saud's own Bedouins gave up in the middle of the fight, only to return once the battle was decided: The Leopard took note of this fact, and was determined not to let this happen again. With regard to al-Duwaish, and rather incredibly, he forgave him again, still trying to win the warlike Mutair over to his side. This new way of treating both his followers and enemies – passing sentence of punishment on them for their misdeeds, but then pardoning them shortly before the punishment's imposition – would soon bring him benefits by generating a current of gratitude towards ibn Saud that would translate into lifelong fidelity most of the time. The Leopard was thus maturing into someone more temperate, flexible, and practical, cutting the circle of family vendettas so common in the Middle East.

Faisal al-Duwaish (or 'al-Daweesh'), in a portrait hand-drawn by a British officer. In the words of Glubb he was not very attractive, *"resembling an ogre"*. He led the rebellion of Qasim against the Saudis in 1907 and betrayed ibn Saud no less than four times. He was forgiven thrice: only his leadership of the rebellion by the Ikhwan fanatics in 1929, proved too much for The Leopard. (Squadron Leader Stewart, via Glubb)

Table 5: Battle of Truffiyah, 22 September 1907

Emirate	Allied Forces	Notes
Shammar/Rashidi		between 3,000 and 4,000 led by ibn Hamud
	Shammar levies	
	Buraida levies	
	Mutair Bedouin	al-Duwaish
Riyadh/Saud		around 5,000 led by ibn Saud
	Arid levies	
	Qahtan Bedouin	
	'Ataiba Bedouin	
	Subai Bedouin	
	Suhul Bedouin	

In the meantime, the Rashidis fled to Buraida, and from there to Häil, their capital. Again in 1908, a newly appointed Emir Rashidi would be assassinated, and replaced by another Rashidi – one with a confusing name: Saud ibn Hamud. Meanwhile, ibn Saud's troops marched on Buraida, only to find that the locals had revolted again. On 29 May 1908, The Leopard managed to get some of his supporters to open the doors to him during the evening prayer, thus securing the town again. True to his new policy, ibn Saud allowed the governor to leave with his family, and appointed Ahmed ibn Mohammed al Sudairi in his stead: a relative of one of his wives. Meanwhile, the Rashidi tribe negotiated a truce in its own internal struggle, and a new leader prevailed: Zamil ibn Subhan. At the battle of Ashaalan, however, Subhan was defeated by the now highly experienced ibn Saud, whilst running an expedition into the latter's territory.[9]

THE DROUGHT CARRYING NEW ENEMIES

At that point in time, ibn Saud was forced to stop his war against the Rashidis for a reason outside his power: a drought in central Nejd. It was to last for several years. Further to the north, in the Shammar lands of the Rashidis, paradoxically, rains were abundant. The result was bad for the Saudi ruler: poverty and hunger increased rebellions in his lands. The worst erupted in al-Hariq, between February and April 1909, where Emir al-Hazzani was killed by members of his own clan. Ibn Saud barely managed to pacify the region. However, these events did not prevent him from contacting the Rwala of Nuri ibn Shaalan, to the northwest (near the modern-day border with Jordan), to continue fighting the Rashidis indirectly, attacking them from behind. Thus, ibn Shaalan snatched the oasis of Jawla, creating a new front against ibn Saud's enemies.

Meanwhile, a few months earlier, in October-November 1908, the Ottomans appointed Hussein ibn Ali as the new Sharif (or Sherif) of Mecca. To win over his new masters, the Sharif collaborated with them in the subjugation of the rebellious region of Asir, while the Ottomans fought a little further south with elements of their 13th and 14th divisions (VII Army), to crush the revolt of Yemen. On his return, the Sharif marched inland, through the oases of Bisha, Ranya and Turaba, which he subdued

Hussein ibn Ali, appointed by the Ottomans Sharif of Mecca in 1908: he became the ruler of the Hejaz, expelling the Ottomans during the Great War, but in turn became the arch rival of ibn Saud in the struggle for the control of Arabia. (Storrs, 1937, via Sander)

and added to his territories, expanding his borders eastwards, approaching dangerously towards the lands of ibn Saud. In fact, these lands would become the initial focus of conflicts with the Sauds that started in 1918-1919. The Sharif Hussein, head of the family clan of the Hashemites, would eventually become ibn Saud's main rival after the defeat of the Rashidis.[10]

3

EMERGENCE OF THE IKHWAN, 1910–1914

Despite attempts by Kuwait's Emir Mubarak to limit the power of the Sauds *vis-à-vis* the Rashidi, ibn Saud, grateful for how Mubarak welcomed his family through the hard times of exile, maintained his friendship with him. His visit to Kuwait in March 1910 was probably aiming to confirm that alliance, from which we have the instance of the first photos taken of ibn Saud and his family. The photographer was Captain William Henry Irvine Shakespear, sent by Cox as British representative to Kuwait. Shakespear and ibn Saud would become friends. Indeed, thanks to the Briton, ibn Saud would have his first contacts with Western culture and technological advances, which he would not hesitate to introduce into his kingdom despite its ultraconservative character. In time, the captain would become a kind of Lawrence of Arabia to the Sauds.

THE ALLIANCE WITH KUWAIT AND THE ARAIF REBELLION

In May 1910, ibn Saud honoured his alliance with Mubarak of Kuwait by sending an army from Riyadh to help him fight the Muntafiq tribe from Mesopotamia, which was ravaging his lands from the north. However, on 16 June, the allied Saudi-Kuwaiti army was defeated at Hadiya by the Muntafiq of Sadoon Pasha, aided by the Rashidis. Taking advantage of Saud's absence, the Araif, a Saudi family branch, left Riyadh to join the Ajmans in al-Hasa, to the east. Once there, they provoked a rebellion claiming the throne of the Nedj. In early 1911, the Araifs and Ajmans marched to Qasim, near Anaiza, where they clashed with Saud's followers. Seeing that the latter were very numerous, the rebels retreated south of Riyadh, to Kharj, and then even farther south, to al-Hariq, in the Hauta region.

The first picture of ibn Saud's family, taken in Kuwait in 1910 by Captain Shakespear. In the first row, from left to right, seated are ibn Saud, his son Turki, Mubarak of Kuwait (and above him Sa´ad, younger brother of ibn Saud), and then Mohammed, half-brother of ibn Saud. (Photo by Shakespear 1910, via Sander)

There, they joined the Hazzani, another tribal rebel group from the southern tip of the Nejd who had been arrested by ibn Saud four years earlier for abusing several of his relatives.

Seeing how the rebellion was beginning to gain weight in the south of the Nejd, ibn Saud sent his brother Sa´ad to raise an army of Bedouins among the 'Ataiba (or Utaibah), to the west, between Riyadh and Mecca. There now reappeared another character key to the fate of Saudi Arabia: the new Sharif of Mecca, Hussein ibn Ali, father of the Hashemites, from whom the current Jordanian royal house (and the former Iraqi royal house) descends. He would be a bitter enemy of the Sauds. The Sharif Hussein considered himself protector of the region of Qasim. As a large number of the caravans that went or came from Mecca passed through there, he demanded that ibn Saud recognize himself as his feudatory and pay him tribute. Seeing how Sa'ad was approaching his territory, he invaded the Nejd and captured him at Qai'iya, 160km southeast of Medina, demanding a ransom. In the autumn, ibn Saud agreed to pay 6,000 Maria Theresia Thalers (about 600 GBP) every year as tribute for Qasim, but once the first payment was made and his brother Sa'ad was released, he reneged on the agreement.

At the same time, ibn Saud marched with a light force of 1,200 to al-Hariq, in the region of Hauta, falling by surprise on the rebels Araif and Hazzani, who had not yet been able to form an army. When he was crossing the Hauta region, south of Riyadh, he discovered that his local governor had already captured one of the Arafi rebels, Saud ibn Abdullah, in Laila. The rest of the Araif fled to Mecca, to the land of their new ally the Sharif Hussein. The Hazzani had worse luck, and 18 of them were beheaded. However, some of the Araif were pardoned, according to The Leopard's new policy. Saud ibn Abdullah and Saud al Kabir, also an Ajman on the mother's side, were grateful, would remain faithful to ibn Saud for the rest of their lives. In fact, the likely ringleader of the rebellion, al-Kabir would marry Nura, ibn Saud's favourite sister, as an attempt to unite both Saudi branches, and also to appease the still-rebellious Ajman. The manoeuvre only partially worked, as the Ajmans would intermittently continue their rebellion until 1916.

This campaign, caused by the severe droughts that were considered by the Bedouins as a sign of having lost the favour of Allah, ended the internal uprisings that threatened the leadership of ibn Saud between 1909 and 1910. Now ibn Saud would return to his campaigns of conquest, but for this he needed to improve his army

Sheikh Mubarak of Kuwait, who – despite his tricks and duplicities (he fomented the Araif rebellion) – was a friend, teacher and ally of ibn Saud. (Photo by Shakespear 1911, via Sander)

Kuwaiti Bedouin warriors. Notable are their dark robes that vividly contrast with the ever white of the Sauds. (RAF Museum)

first. A brief hiatus came when Sheikh Mubarak of Kuwait asked ibn Saud to attack a common enemy, the Zafir tribe of Mesopotamia, in early 1911. As so often, Mubarak practiced a double game and warned the Sheikh of the Zafir, ibn Suwait, of the coming attack. The reason was that he had personal ambitions for Qasim, Washm and Sudair, so he was interested in weakening both the Zafir and the Sauds. Ibn Suwait, in turn, informed ibn Saud, who continued to maintain the performance, calling the leader of Kuwait 'father' (in turn, Mubarak called ibn Saud his, 'son').

The Ottomans, already having their hands full fighting the Italian invasion of Libya, now faced a new uprising in the area of Asir, this time by the Idrisis. Consequently, they demanded help from Saud – which he refused. Soon after, in 1912, and probably as a punishment for ibn Saud's rejection, the Hashemites of the Sharif Hussein of Mecca – who remained a loyal Ottoman subject – sent a section of ´Ataiba to plunder the western area of the Nejd. Ibn Saud's brother, Mohammed, responded by attacking the pro-Hashemite ´Ataiba. The Sharif in turn retaliated by forbidding the Sauds to perform the November-December *hajj* or peregrination to Mecca. This was a blow to Saudi merchants, as a large source of income was produced during these celebrations. Clearly, the rivalry between Sauds and Hashemites was now to reach its peak.[1]

THE FOUNDATION OF THE WARRIOR MONKS: THE IKHWAN

During the ten years of conquest that began in 1902, the Sauds always had a feudal army formed by two components: the citizen militias and the Bedouin cavalry. The militias had always behaved well in combat and had never betrayed their master. However, they were not very mobile troops and, as Saudi dominions expanded, it was increasingly difficult to call them to service. They had to re-deploy to ever more distant fronts, and then return to their cities of origin, mainly Riyadh, to attend to their crops, families, and businesses.

A Maria Theresia Thaler. (Sander's collection)

By contrast, the Bedouins, more agile, mounted on camels and horses, and knowledgeable of life in the desert were easier to summon, to move from one place to another and to attend to all fronts. The problem was that the Bedouins fought mostly for booty, so they often abandoned the expedition if there was no clear prospect of obtaining any, or simply neglected the fight to fall on enemy camps and loot them. In addition, they did not hesitate to defect or change sides in the middle of a fight if it benefited their own local interests, or to avenge for an affront. Furthermore, the Bedouins tended to avoid combat and clashes, focusing only on skirmishes or surprise attacks, to reduce their casualties and risk to life.

Faced with this dilemma, ibn Saud realized that he needed the Bedouins to fight, but also that they had to be loyal to him, and to abandon the custom of pillage. To do this, he decided to make them sedentary, like the urban militias, and replace the national fervour – non-existent anyway in the Arab tribal lands – with religious fervour. This was why he began applying Wahhabism as a unifying element and the germ of a national consciousness based on the branch of Islam considered as exclusive and proper by the Sauds. This was not a desperate move or lacked calculation: ibn Saud was related through marriage with the descendants of the founder of this Muslim doctrine, Abdul Wahhab, and his own troops of citizen militias were already followers of this tenet. Thus, ibn Saud would turn his Bedouin tribes into fanatical warrior-monks. They would live in their own communities, like medieval convents. They would be a kind of Arab Knights Templar, as an idea for comparison, and they would be known as the Brotherhood, or Ikhwan.

IKHWAN TRIBES AND CONVENTS

To affect such a reform, ibn Saud sent his Wahhabi missionaries to the *Mutawwa'in*, to preach among the Bedouins. Also, he distributed tools, seeds, and economic aid to cultivate the lands, to make the Bedouins farmers, and he grouped them in communities or *Hujar* (convents) from where it would be easier to locate them and call to arms. The initiators of this movement, supported by ibn Saud, were Muhammad ibn Abd al-Latif, the *Qadhi* of Riyadh; Sheikh Isa, the *Qadhi* of Al-Hasa; and Abd-al-Karim al-Maghrebi, coming from North Africa and settled in Artawiya, future first base of the Ikhwan.

Thus, the first community - or *Hujar* - was founded specifically in the lands of the Mutair, north of Riyadh and east of Qasim, in the wells of Artawiya, in 1912, and under the doubly rebellious and doubly forgiven Faisal al-Duwaish. Before long, the first Ikhwan were joined by the Uraimat or Araimat section of the Harb or Harab tribe. Shortly afterwards a third community would be founded southwest of Riyadh, in Ghaghat, within the tribe of 'Ataiba (Utaibah). It was controlled by Sheikh Sultan ibn Bijud ibn Humaid (colloquially ibn Bijad) and located between the Saudi capital and the lands of the Hejaz under the Sharif Hussein of Mecca. Convinced by the preaching of the Wahhabi missionaries and the generous donations for their maintenance, more and more Bedouins joined the Ikhwan. These were paid once a year by ibn Saud and then by the Amirs of each convent, depending on the number of followers recruited. Specifically, the communities were founded to watch over the enemies of the Sauds: The Ikhwan of Mutair under al-Duwaish would watch over the Rashidis, to the north, and the Ottomans, to the east; the Harb, under ibn Nuhait, in Duhna, would watch over the Shammaries, the Iraqi tribes, and the Hejazis, to the west, north and southwest respectively; those of the 'Ataiba, under ibn Bijad, from their seat of Ghaghat, were to keep in check the Hejaz, to the west. The Ajman, since 1915, with their convent of Sarrar or As-Sarar, would guard Kuwait and the coast of the Persian Gulf, to the north and east; and finally, since their submission in 1921-22, the Shammaries – ex-Rashidis under ibn Jibril and ibn Thunaiyan – at their headquarters in Al-Akhfar, were tasked with keeping tribes of Mesopotamia in the north at bay.

By 1920 there were 52 Hijras/Hujars, or convents; that became 72 in 1923; and about 120 by 1929 (at the time of their rebellion against ibn Saud). According to some sources numbers reached up to 200 Hujars or convents, adding up to about 150,000 adult males. Despite that terrific number, not all of them were potential warriors for ibn Saud. There were, artisans, merchants, builders, and similar professions were, but these were considered ignoble, and had to supply their labour, food, and clothing to the warriors of the Ikhwan. Even warriors were divided into three categories: those who were always ready for war; reservists, summoned only in case of necessity; and those who always remained in the convents to defend them and only fought in exceptional circumstances. In 1929, they were distributed as follows:

- Anaza: 7 convents;
- Shammar: 16 convents;
- Harb: 22 convents;
- Mutair: 12 convents;
- 'Ataiba: 15 convents;

A very young (still lacking the typical beard) Ikhwan warrior in 1923. Notable is his open *turban*, wrapped around the head, white and plain – very typical on the Ikhwan. Below it he wore the *Keffiyeh* with red pattern on the white cloth, typical for many Arab tribes. Interestingly, this one wore no *agal* (black ropes with knots that held the turbans of the Arab Bedouins): this was another sign of being an Ikhwan. Also notable is his relatively short robe, not reaching the floor and showing the boots – another characteristics for the Ikhwan. He is armed with a Mauser rifle, a large knife with a richly decorated scabbard, and, almost hidden to the right, a sword. (via Almana)

- Subai: 3 convents;
- Suhul: 3 convents;
- Qahtan: 8 convents;
- Dawasir: 4 convents;
- Beni Khalid: 2 convents;
- Ajman: 14 convents (there was a plan for 22),
- Awazim: 2 convents;
- Bani Hajir: 4 convents;
- al-Murra: 4 convents;
- Hitaim: 3 convents; and
- Zafir: 1 convent.

If one assigned a flag to each of the convents, and calculated about 100 warriors per flag, this would have given ibn Saud a total of 12,000 combatants at his permanent disposal. Of these, the larger Mutair, 'Ataiba, Shammar, Harb, and Ajman convents probably provided between 1,000 and 2,000 warriors, while the rest totalled only a few hundred.

Table 6: Ikhwan Tribes of the 1910s-1920s

Tribe	Number of Convents	Warriors (estimates)
'Ataiba/Utaiba	15	1,500
Ajman	14 or 22	1,400-2,200
Anaza	7	700
Awazim	2	200
Bani Hajir	4	400
Bani Khalid	2	200
Dawasir	4	400
Harb/Harab	22	2,200
Hitaim	3	300
Murra	4	400
Mutair	12	1,200
Qahtan	8	800
Shammar	16	1,600
Subai	3	300
Suhul	3	300
Zafir	1	100

A TOOL OF WAR

Even by the standards of the most conservative sects of Islam, the customs of the Ikhwan were tremendously puritanical. They advocated the forced conversion of their followers and forbade the use of silk and luxurious dress. They also forbade music, gambling, jewellery, and, of course, tobacco and alcohol. As for physical appearance, their robes were not to touch the ground; and men were not to groom excessively long beards or moustaches. They wore a turban that was open on the top (not closed, like on other Arabs), and this had to be white and plain, unlike the turbans of other Sauds, who usually wore turbans Keffiyeh, with a red pattern drawn on the white cloth, rolled over the cloth of the head. The Ikhwan never wore the *agal* (the typical black rope with knots, that held turbans in position). Tremendously intolerant, those caught not complying with these rules were beaten and exhibited in public. On a visit to the Artawiya convent, they even told ibn Saud himself that his dress was too long: eventually, scissors passed from hand to hand and proceeded to cut the King's clothes while he was still wearing them.

In war, unlike Bedouin customs, the Ikhwan did not accept – nor respect – prisoners, and frequently had no mercy for women or children. They were, however, imbued with a great moral superiority for their faith, and they were as skilled in warfare as the Bedouins, but also as constant and obedient as the citizen militias. They were not distracted by anything from prayer and war. Developing a culture of martyrdom in order to enter Paradise, they proved fierce fighters, tremendously effective in combat. In battle they were to be recognized by their large green flags with text in Arabic, 'There is no God but Allah' (La illah il Ullah), and with their main troop of camel riders always in the centre, flanked by riders on horseback, and followed by footmen running behind the mounts, bellowing their cry '*the wind of Paradise is blowing, where are you looking for it?*'

At first, they were armed only with staffs, spears, and swords, but later, throughout the Great War, they were armed with rifles captured from their enemies – like Ottoman Mausers - and with Lee Enfield SMLE MK IIIs supplied by the British. Regardless, they always wore a knife or sword in their belt, along with a bandolier. Any booty was distributed with a fifth being allocated to ibn Saud, and the rest to the Ikhwan. Over time they went from being auxiliaries, in 1914, to becoming the bulk of Saudi troops after 1918. Their tactics, based on careful reconnaissance and surprise attacks at dawn after night marches over up to 100 kilometres, has already been described in the Chapter 1. With this shock force, ibn Saud would finish the conquest of almost the entire Arab Peninsula. The aggressiveness and intolerance of the Ikhwan would soon bring him problems, however, which Saud tried to control as best as possible. For example, the Ikhwan had to be ordered not to disturb their Shi'a subjects, present in al-Hasa, east of Riyadh, all the way to the coast of the Persian Gulf. Moreover, in 1919, ibn Saud forbade the forced conversion practiced by the Ikhwan.[2]

ENTER CAPTAIN SHAKESPEAR

As the Nejd was isolated in the middle of Arabia, ibn Saud urgently needed access to the sea to be able to communicate with other powers, boost his trade and import products from the West – especially the rifles, machine guns, cannons and ammunition his autarkic regime required to survive. To do this, the easiest action would be to occupy the lands of al-Hasa, east of Riyadh. This region included tribes of the Shi'a sect, and was protected by an Ottoman garrison. In addition, the land was rich in oases and provided attractive customs revenues precisely because of the entry of goods that were imported from further afar via the ports of the Persian Gulf. Therefore, and recalling his chats with Captain Shakespear in Kuwait, and aiming to avoid retaliation from Constantinople, ibn Saud decided to first ask for the protection of another great power. It was for this purpose, on 7 March 1911, he summoned Captain Shakespear to his desert camp outside Thaj.

Over just three days, the friendship between these two men greatly deepened. Being sincere, Shakespear warned him that, in principle, London did not want to alter the status quo with the Ottoman Empire. During this stay he took some impressive photographs of the Saudi army on camelback, with their green flags displayed in the desert, and of ibn Saud´s family (see Chapters 2 and 3). After a severe reprimand for having contacted Saud without permission from his government, Shakespear returned to Kuwait in January 1912 (he also desired to get away from a woman who had caused him a bout of lovesickness). Then, in 1913, Shakespear departed for an expedition to cross the desert, to Majma'a where, he had learned, his friend ibn Saud was in Khafs. On 30 March 1912, he went to see him. It remains unknown what the Captain and the Emir talked about. During this time, the otherwise meticulous British officer did not leave behind any kind of record (for example in his diary). However, only a month and five days after this meeting, ibn Saud attacked al-Hasa. As was expected, this caused Shakespear to quarrel with London, but it is possible that the British Resident in the Gulf,

Captain William Shakespear, British liaison in Kuwait. He would become a friend of ibn Saud, advising him how to attack the Ottomans without breaking with the British Empire. An adventurer and a photographer, he took the first known pictures of ibn Saud and his family, and of an Arab army on the move. (Winstone, via Sander)

Sir Percy Zachary Cox, secretly supported him – or at least tolerated his action. One way or the other, Cox had to deal with the angry reaction of ibn Saud and Mubarak of Kuwait because of the 'British support for the Ottomans'. It is possible that Shakespear informed ibn Saud that his invasion of al-Hasa would not provoke a strong reaction from the British, and may even have given him some advice on how to conduct the campaign. Eventually, this 'show of support' ended up winning the Brit a friend in the heart of ibn Saud.

OTTOMAN EXPULSION FROM AL-HASA

With the Ottoman Empire having been defeated by Italy in Libya, and then embroiled in the First Balkan War, ibn Saud's move for action in al-Hasa could not have been better timed. The Ottoman governor of the Vilayet Baghdad, Jamal Pasha, received intelligence of the Saudi intentions and threatened to send two battalions to the Nejd, but ibn Saud responded that he would make the walk more bearable by approaching them with his army. Following this typical exchange, during the night from 4 to 5 May 1913, covered by palm groves, 800 militiamen led by ibn Saudi in person, approached the 10-metres-tall, mud and stone walls of Hofuf, the capital of al-Hasa. They carefully scouted the defences, and saw not only a moat protecting the wall, but also three isolated forts that defended access, and the five well-defended gates. Finally, they discovered a section of the wall in the north, which was about 300 metres long and included no towers: essentially, this was unprotected except by the citadel (*al-Kut*), located in the middle of the city.

On the basis of these scouting reports, ibn Saud decided to attack this section of the wall. Under cover of the night, he sent 20 warriors equipped with palm tree trunks and ropes to climb the fortification and then advance undetected through the esplanade – as they had done at Riyadh in 1902. Once up, they descended inside the city and then opened the southern gate, aided by some Algosaibis - merchants

Ibn Saud and his family, as photographed by Shakespear at Thaj, in 1911. Visible in the rear row, second from left, is Sa´ad, brother of ibn Saud; ibn Saud is seated, surrounded by some of his sons. To his left is his half-brother Mohammed. (Photo by Shakespear 1911, via Almana)

from Bahrain in the pay of ibn Saud. The bulk of the force then charged through the gate, first attacking the Ottoman Army barracks and then the al-Kut: their assault was supported by the population, much of which turned out to be against the Ottoman presence. Totally surprised, the garrison was de-facto overrun: only a few managed to take refugee inside the citadel. Another group escaped to the Mosque of Ibrahim Pasha, but ended up surrendering at sunset when the Sauds warned them they would blow up a mine underneath the building. Following several hours of negotiations, the rest of the garrison followed in fashion; 1,200 Mutasarrif Ottomans under Nadim Bey surrendered, were marched to the port of Oqair, 100 kilometres east, and embarked ships that brought them to Bahrain. The Leopard now had possession of his first port.

Hofuf, capital of al-Hasa, with its mud walls and its moat protecting the access to the town. (Sander, 1940)

The Mosque of Ibrahim Pasha peeping over the walls of Hofuf. The remnants of the Ottoman garrison took refugee inside this building, before surrendering to ibn Saud under the threat that a mine was going to be blown up underneath them. (Sander, 1940)

Another view of Hofuf, protected by towers. The north sector, where there were none, was where ibn Saud infiltrated during his night assault. (Sander, 1940)

The expulsion of the Ottomans from al-Hasa resulted in the garrisons of Dammam, Jubail, and Qatif – about 90 troops in total – fleeing to Bahrain as well. Ibn Saud quickly exploited the opportunity to seize all three. Superficially, the Ottomans were not ready to give up just like this. They embarked a battalion of their army troops on a British ship in Basra and sent it to Bahrain with a plan to then attempt to recover Qatif and Oqair. However, the troops did not even try to land.

The Leopard appointed ibn Jiluwi – his fierce cousin who had stormed Riyadh with him in 1902 – as governor of al-Hasa. Under Saud, the province – which used to pay 37,000 lire to Baghdad, but which in turn actually cost Constantinople up to 52,000 lire to pay and keep the thousand Ottoman soldiers garrisoning the province, and so was, in actual fact, in deficit – began to increase its income: this even more so once the Sauds expelled foreign merchants, replaced them with locals and began taxing all imported goods at 8%. What ibn Saud could not know at the time was that exactly in this region, in al-Hasa, in 1938, some of largest oil reserves of the world were to be discovered, changing the whole Arab world once and forever.

BETWEEN THE BRITISH AND THE OTTOMANS

Following the failed Ottoman counterattacks – and these from the territories claimed as British protectorates – ibn Saud complained to Cox, and in turn Cox complained to ibn Saud. Ironically, at the same time, the ruler in Riyadh also wrote a letter to the Sultan in Constantinople, stressing he was remaining loyal, and had 'only' recovered the lands of his ancestors. This was rather unsurprising. In theory, at least, ibn Saud's position was very weak, as he was at the mercy of two great powers. Indeed, he was squeezed between them. However, in practice, both the British and the Ottoman Empires were preoccupied with developments far away from the Arabian Peninsula, and not interested in launching any kind of large-scale conquests in that area. Unsurprisingly, while Cox initially refused to deal with Saud again, Eduard Grey, Foreign Secretary of the government in London, gave his permission to contact the Saudi ruler because, on 29 July 1913, London and Constantinople signed the Anglo-Ottoman Convention. At the time of growing tensions in Europe, this aimed to preserve peace and distance the Sultan from the Central Powers. Moreover, on 11 September 1913, Cox informed ibn Saud that if he respected the integrity of other sheikdoms in the Persian Gulf, London would mediate in his favour with the Sultan. In turn, The Leopard demanded guarantees that there would be no Ottoman retaliation. Therefore, on 15-16 December 1913, Cox sent Shakespear to Oqair, for negotiations with ibn Saud. These ended fruitlessly, because London could not issue the guarantees Saud wanted. Much to the surprise of the Saudi ruler, however, the Sultan then reacted by making a particularly attractive offer. Determined to secure his southern flank amid the imminence of the Great War, and keen to avoid having a pro-British kingdom within the territories of his empire, he offered ibn Saud to appoint the Wali (governor) of the Nejd. He also promised Saud deliveries of arms and ammunition, in exchange for renouncing his right to having independent foreign policy, and to side with the Ottoman Empire in the case of war. The only negative conditions were that the Sauds had to tolerate the presence of Ottoman garrisons in al-Hasa and not allow any foreign merchants to operate from territories under their control.

The British were displeased by this offer, because they were keen to have their merchants in local ports and to negotiate with ibn Saud on their own. Therefore, London attempted to force Constantinople to withdraw this agreement and requested ibn Saud to delay his response by three months. In the meantime, on 9 March 1914, the British sent Shakespear to talk with The Leopard again.

The British Resident in the Persian Gulf, Sir Percy Zachary Cox. Cox would try to keep a delicate balance between the Ottomans and ibn Saud, in order to help the second but not forcing a break with Constantinople on the eve of the Great War. Later, trusted by ibn Saud for being an 'honest man', he would draw the frontiers (his famous red line) between Iraq, Kuwait and Arabia in the Oqair Protocol of 1922. (via Sander)

Ibn Saud, however, felt he had no clarity over his own situation at that point. He only knew that the Ottomans were still sending arms and ammunitions to his enemies, the Rashidis, and calculated that Constantinople could still lunch a counterattack from the sea to recover al-Hasa. His uncertainty went so far as to lead him to order the mobilisation of his army. Simultaneously, London, keen to avoid driving the Ottomans into German hands, decided to leave the ruler in Riyadh on his own. Thus, ibn Saud was free to conclude related negotiations largely along the offers of the Sultan, though including the condition of an Ottoman garrison in al-Hasa. The treaty contained only one additional clause: the number of soldiers stationed there was to be agreed on an annual basis between the Sauds and the local Ottoman commander. Thus, thanks to the impending risks of the Great War in Europe, there was no retaliation for the conquest of al-Hasa, and on 29 May 1914, the Ottoman Wali of Basra signed an agreement with ibn Saud.[3]

However, in July 1914, Constantinople then ordered ibn Saud that in the case of war he should march with his army to defend Basra against the British. In exchange he would receive arms and money. Subsequently, now well-versed in such machinations, ibn Saud reported this order to the British, in turn extracting a promise of British support from the new Resident for the Persian Gulf, Knox (Cox had been assigned to the army that was about to invade Basra), for the case of an Ottoman counter-invasion from the sea. Even more important was the fact that Knox promised the recognition of Saud's independence if he cooperated in the capture of Basra with Mubarak of Kuwait, and if he helped prevent the arrival of the Ottoman reinforcements.

As it was subsequently learned, the Ottomans were actually trying to buy time. Through the summer of 1914, they developed a plan to send the 1st Battalion of their 29th Regiment (8th Division from Tekirdağ-Rodosto) to recover al-Hasa, and then spearhead a campaign into the Saudi-controlled territories. This was to be initiated in October 1914. Only the outbreak of the First World War, and then the Ottoman entry into that conflict on the side of the Central Powers, on 29 October 1914, prevented this offensive.

4

THE GREAT WAR, 1914–1918

As the above-described negotiations were going on, in early February 1914, Captain Shakespear – now 35 years old, and still in love with adventure – began an excursion to cross the desert, that also served as an excuse to secretly meet ibn Saud. After crossing 2,800 kilometres, on 17 May he reached Kuntilla in the eastern Sinai, in Egypt. From there, he travelled to London, where he pressed for recognition of Saudi sovereignty and independence. Preoccupied with developments in Europe, London did not react. When the Great War erupted, Shakespear was sent back to the Middle East, this time as officially appointed British representative to ibn Saud's court, with the task of convincing Riyadh to side with the British. Now the leader of the Sauds was caught between two contradictory offers (those of the Ottomans and of the British), the question became: which steps should he take in order to survive?

Captain William Shakespear, who assisted Saud's warriors during the battle of Jarrab against the Rashidies. He was to lose his life trying to protect the Saud's artillery crew from a cavalry attack. Ibn Saud, impressed, and a true friend, would later say that he was the greatest Western man that he had ever known. (via Sander)

SHAKESPEAR: THE LAWRENCE ON THE SAUDI SIDE

Shakespear met ibn Saud on 31 December 1914, north of the Ikhwan convent of Artawiya, of the Mutair tribe of al-Duwaish. The Leopard set up his camp about 75 kilometres east of Buraida. Significantly, Shakespear's return to Arabia took place more than a year-and-a-half before that of Thomas E Lawrence – and he was meeting the actual decision maker.

Over the following days, the two negotiated the draft text of an alliance between the Sauds and the British Empire, which the Captain sent to Cox in mid-January. While that was going on, ibn Saud's army of about 6,000 began preparing for battle. The only reason he had not acted earlier was his wish to get rid of his archenemies: the Rashidis. Among his troops of early 1915 were about 1,500 natives of el-Aridh (Riyadh and environs), about 4,000 Bedouins from the 'Ataiba, Suhul, Suhai, and Harb tribes, the Ikhwan of Mutair of Artawiya, and some Ajman horsemen. As the preparations reached their peak, ibn Saud urged Shakespear not to risk his life but to return to Kuwait. However, the Captain refused. He wanted to be present at this battle between the Arabs and to photograph one of these clashes for the first time. Ultimately, his great passion for photography was to cost him his life.

THE BATTLE OF JARRAB

At dawn on 24 January 1915, ibn Saud's army collided with the Rashidis in the Jarrab area, north of the Qasim region, and in the town of Zilfi. Led by Saud ibn Salih – the new Emir of Häil –, the Rashidis numbered around 4,000, including 1,500 from Häil's militias. Initially, they attempted to surround ibn Saud's position. Therefore, instead of attacking from the direction of the Shammar in the north, they did so from the southwest. The Sauds, however, detected their approach. They deployed a line of riflemen along the northern side of the Wadi ar-Rumah dry river, with their flanks protected by cavalry and camel-riders. The Ajmans were on the left flank. Behind the line, on a sand hill, stood the Saud's sole artillery piece: an Ottoman gun captured in 1904. Positioned alongside this, in his uniform of the 17th Bengali Lancers, was Captain Shakespear – armed with a pistol and immortalising the battle with his camera.

Aiming to surprise the Sauds, the Rashidis marched along the dry riverbed – until they ran into the trap: the Sauds discharged their fire into the enemy's left flank and then charged them. At that point in time, Shakespear observed the enemy reserve and ordered the gunners to shell it. In between, the battle raged on and the Sauds – reinforced by their cavalry – began pushing the Rashidis back. Simultaneously, the infantry of the Shammaris and Häil forced back the Saud infantry from the Nejd. As the battle developed, the Ajmans realised that the Rashidi camp further south was almost defenceless. They abandoned their position on the left flank and rushed to plunder. Although being shelled, the Rashidi reserve saw the opportunity offering itself, and galloped into the gap left by the Ajmans. They attacked the Saud infantry from the flank, overwhelming it. When the Rashidi infantry began assaulting the sand hill, atop of which was the sole gun, the Saudi gunners dismounted, buried the breechblock and shouted at Shakespear to flee. However, the captain was determined to cover the retreat of his companions. He drew his pistol and shot at the attackers. He continued shooting even after being hit by a bullet in the leg, and until the Rashidi camel-riders wounded him in the arm and then shot him in the head, killing the British officer. Worse than the death of his close friend, and as a further result of the Ajmans leaving their position, ibn Saud's army was beaten in the Battle of Jarrab. Fortunately for The Leopard, the Rashidis suffered such heavy losses that they could not exploit this victory: each side lost around 100 killed.

Table 7: Battle of Jarrab, 24 January 1915

Emirate	Allied Forces	Strength	Notes
Shammar/Rashidi		4,000	led by Saud ibn Salih
	Shammar Bedouin		
	Häil Militia	(1,500)	Included in the total strength
Nejd & Hasa/Saud		6,000	led by ibn Saud
	el-Aridh & Royal levies	(1,500)	Included in the total strength
	'Ataiba/Utaiba Bedouin		
	Suhul Bedouin		
	Suhai Bedouin		
	Harb Bedouin		
	Mutair		Ikhwan of Artawiya
	Ajman Bedouin		mounted on horses

Despite Shakespear's untimely death, Saud owed much to the Captain: his knowledge of the Western world and his first agreements with the English, and the germ of British recognition of Saud independence were all due to him. However, if Shakespear was Lawrence's predecessor, he was also his antithesis. Notwithstanding that his contact and work were much shorter, and thus of less overall influence: unlike Lawrence, he never adopted Arab dress or customs, bathed whenever he could, continued eating European style, as well as drinking wine and whisky when alone. That being said, he was quite similar to ibn Saud in his appearance: young, tall, strong, somewhat authoritarian, but also generous, virile, direct and frank, incapable of any duplicity. Their physical similarities were also accompanied by shared hobbies: Shakespear enjoyed hunting with falcons and salukis, as did ibn Saud. All this resulted in a deep and real friendship. In 1927, when someone asked The Leopard who was the greatest Westerner he had ever met, he answered without hesitation: '*Captain Shakespear*'.[1]

FIGHT AGAINST THE AJMAN

Shakespear's services, even in the short term, were of tremendous worth. On the eve of the Battle of Jarrab, a Hejazi army commanded by Abdullah, the eldest son of Sharif Hussein of Mecca, invaded the Nejd and reached Shara, southwest of Anaiza, 250km from the site of the battle between the Rashidis and the Sauds. However, at the same time the Hejazis were negotiating their own agreement with the British – aiming to betray the Ottomans (which would lead to the entry on the scene of the 'Lawrence of Arabia', in late 1916). In the course of the negotiations, and as a result of Shakespear's liaison, the British promptly warned them not to push their invasion further as ibn Saud was one of their allies. Frustrated, the Hashemites turned around.

Meanwhile, ibn Saud had another problem to deal with, which – once again – prevented him from joining the British effort against the Ottoman Empire, regardless how dissatisfied he was with his strategic situation. The issue was one of priorities: he could not involve himself in a bigger war without having secured control at home. Not only had the Ajman left the battlefield of Jarrab to plunder the Rashidi camp, some of them were Shi'a. Further, The Leopard's governor, his cousin ibn Jiluwi, was very strict in the application of the Sharia, the Islamic Law, and constantly increasing tax demands. This went so far that the Ajman – supported by the Murra, who lived in the extreme south of habitable Arabia – then rebelled against the Saud's rule. Therefore, in August 1915, ibn Saud and his brother Sa'ad marched with 300 militiamen and 900 Bani Hajir Bedouin from al-Hasa toward the rebellious Ajman. On encountering them in Jebel Kinzan, he entered negotiations. Whether the latter were serious or aiming to buy time to improve their own position, remains unknown. What is known is that Sa'ad proposed ibn Saud ambush the rebels, but his plan was discovered. Not only was Sa'ad killed during the resulting fire-fight, ibn Saud was also slightly wounded by a ricocheting cartridge, while his forces lost 300 dead. As it turned out, he was defeated because the Ajmans had gathered perhaps 2,000 men in total and thus outnumbered both The Leopard's army and ibn Jiluwi's garrison. As a consequence, by October 1915, the survivors had to withdraw and take cover behind the walls of al-Hasa's capital, Hofuf.

Table 8: Battle of Jebel Kinzan, August 1915

Emirate	Allied Forces	Strength	Notes
Ajman		2,000	
Nejd & Hasa/Saud			led by ibn Saud & Sa'ad
	Militia	300	
	Bani Hajir Bedouin	900	

On receiving reports that ibn Saud was isolated, a relief force under this half-brother Mohammed was gathered in Riyadh. Reinforced by a contingent of Kuwaitis led by Prince Salim (Mubarak's son), this group joined The Leopard in Hofuf, reinforcing him to a degree where he was able to initiate a series of raids into the rebel-held territory. Ibn Saud was wounded in the thigh during one of the operations in question, but as encouragement for his men, he arranged himself a marriage he consummated that same day. Finally, in December 1915, ibn Saud, allied Kuwaitis, and the various warriors from the area he had rallied around himself managed to corner the Ajman in Ridgha, in central al-Hasa – and defeat them, the Araif, and the allied Murra. As Salim's Kuwaitis then returned to Hofuf, however, they argued with Mohammed and became so furious that they abandoned ibn Saud. To make matters worse, Mubarak then offered asylum to the surviving rebels: after 15 years of cordial friendship between ibn Saud and Mubarak, they became archenemies.

Despite this, late 1915 was not all bad news for The Leopard. On 26 December, he met Sir Percy Cox on Tarut Island, near Qatif (in the territory of ibn Saud's allies Bani Hajir). There, the two finally signed the agreement arranged by Shakespear in the now seeming distant January. Henceforth, the British Crown recognised ibn Saud

Sa'ad ibn Saud, the handsome younger brother of ibn Saud, in a picture taken by Shakespear at Thaj in 1911. Sa´ad lost his life when trying to ambush the Ajman during a negotiation in 1915. (Shakespear 1911, via Almana)

as Emir of Nejd and al-Hasa – but with several conditions. He was prohibited from signing any kind of agreements with other nations, he had to keep the routes to Medina and Mecca open for everybody, and he was prohibited from attacking territories under the British protection. The Sauds thus converted from being a quasi-Ottoman-protectorate to becoming a de-facto British protectorate.

As a gratuity for this arrangement, ibn Saud also received British-supplied weaponry. He requested 3,000 rifles (thus probably indicating the strength of his standing force), but Cox provided only 300 Mausers captured from the Ottomans, and these arrived in spring of 1916. It was only in June of that year that the British met the original request and delivered 3,000 of their own rifles. With this armament and a loan of GBP 20,000, ibn Saud was now finally able to expel the last Ajman rebels from al-Hasa, driving them all the way to Kuwait. The Ajman remained hostile to the Sauds to the degree whereby The Leopard subsequently dissolved what was left of the tribe into two dozens of Ikhan hijras or Ikhwan convents, scattered throughout the Nejd (probably indicating the Ajman were capable of putting around 2,000 warriors under arms). [2]

THE RISE OF THE HASHEMITES

Whilst not the subject of this text, at this point there is the need to outline the overall flow of political and military developments to the west of the part of the Arabian Peninsula now controlled by the Sauds. This is because, while ibn Saud was distracted by the need to counter a major uprising in his rear, Sharif al-Hussein bin Ali al-Hashimi of the Hejaz – the patriarch of the Hashemite family and thus the ruler of Mecca – pursued his own interests, and was soon to become The Leopard's greatest rival for supremacy on the Arabian Peninsula.

Coming from the Banu Qatadah branch of the Banu Hashim clan, Hussein was appointed the Sharif of Mecca by the Ottomans in 1908, in the aftermath of the Young Turk Revolution. However, his relations with Constantinople deteriorated as a result of the new regime's policies of Turkification. In 1914, Hussein made his first move: he sent his son Abdullah to Cairo with the aim of entering negotiations with Field Marshal Lord Kitchener, and to receive economic- and military aid in exchange for rebelling against the Ottomans. At the time, London was preoccupied with the outbreak of the Great War in Europe, and Kitchener was recalled to London, resulting in a standstill. The situation experienced a fundamental change once the Ottoman Empire sided with the Central Powers, and especially after the British defeats at Sinai, Gallipoli, and in Mesopotamia. All of a sudden, at first, small shipments of money and arms began crossing the

The Souk or market place of Hofuf, capital of al-Hasa. Ibn Saud had to take refuge in this town after the Ajman killed his brother Sa´ad. He was only saved by a relief force led by his other brother Mohammed. (Popperfoto, via Almana)

Red Sea, and then finally London realised that Hussein's idea of an 'Arab revolt' was not a bad one.

The fact that by then the waters were muddied by a few other affairs appears not to have disturbed anybody. For example, during a meeting in Ta'if of June 1915, Hussein's decision to contact the British was not entirely welcome by all of his sons: only Abdullah advocated action, while Faisal advised caution, and Ali argued against. In May 1916, the British Empire and France, ratified the secret Sykes-Picot Treaty (and informed the Russian Empire about this agreement), by which they were to defeat the Ottoman Empire and then distribute its territory between themselves and their local allies (the treaty became public when revealed by the Soviets, in the aftermath of the downfall of the Russian Empire). Sykes-Picot not only ignored Sharif Hussein's demands for a unified kingdom of Arabs including not only Hejaz, but all of the Vilayets of Syria, Baghdad and Mosul, it also ignored the emergence of nationalist Arab movements. It also ignored that the majority of the nationalists in question were actually complaining about the Young Turks Revolution of 1908 converting the Sultan – who was also the Caliph of (Sunni) Islam – into a merely symbolic figure, at best.

During the following months, London, aghast by successive defeats at Gallipoli and al-Qut, tried to add new allies through making promises to, amongst others, the Kurds in northern Mesopotamia for their independence, and then to the Zionist movement (foremost in the United States of America) for a National Home in Palestine. Unsurprisingly, Sharif Hussein exploited the opportunity to obtain British recognition of himself as the 'King of the Arabs'. Though, later on, this was followed by a more nuanced proclamation as the 'King of Hejaz', but before it got to this, Great Britain already began backing him with GBP 30,000 a month.

That said, Hussein's decision to launch an uprising was already taken before the British agreed to support him, and thus quite risky – even if launched in quite a demonstrative fashion. Following the call for a morning prayer from the minaret of the Grand Mosque in Mecca, the Sharif picked up a rifle, leaned out of the window of his palace, and fired into the air. In a matter of minutes, his followers – who had arrived the night before in small groups – took up arms and occupied the streets, thus starting the Arab Revolt.[3]

Reportedly, the Hashemites then managed to gather together an army of up to 30,000 warriors. With hindsight, it can be concluded that such reports were wildly exaggerated. Not only was Sharif Hussein at that time only receiving enough money from London (GBP 30,000) to pay for about 9,000 combatants (even half that number, 4,500, if one adds the cost of equipment, arms, ammunition, and food): there is also the fact is that he was unable to recruit more than the citizen militia of Mecca, and then those of Jeddah and Taif – all of whom had very little combat capability (as was to become painfully obvious during the next major war with the Sauds, in 1924-1925, as will be described in Volume 2). These numbers were gradually reinforced by tribal contingents of the Harith, the Bani 'Ali, the Bani 'Atiya, the Bani Salem, the Juhaynah, the 'Ataiba/Utaybah, and the Huweitat. Whilst these were more combat effective, they were fewer in numbers and consisted of the Bedouin fighting for their share of the loot. Moreover, even by the end of 1916, the British had provided only about 10,000 rifles to Hussein. So, this would be the actual number of Hejaz warriors at the beginning of the war: between 4,000 and 9,000 men. This would reach about 10,000-15,000 at the beginning of 1917, at the ratio of 5,000 warriors for each of the three armies operational by the time. The reported 30,000 (or, and more likely, some 26,000) had gathered around him only by late 1918, by when British financial aid had also reached GBP 220,000 a month. These numbers were thanks to the tribes from much more populous Vilayets of Syria and Baghdad, which had joined *en masse* the Hashemites and Lawrence. In fact, in 1924-1925, when Saud faced the Hashemites, and they did not have British help, nor the tribes of northern Arabia on their side, they proved capable of putting only some 3,000 under arms, as will be described in Volume 2. The conclusion is, therefore, that for most of the uprising, at hand, Sharif Hussein, his sons, and Lawrence never led more than about 15,000 warriors at once.[4]

The much-praised 'Arab Revolt' was an ironic affair for a few other reasons, too. It began with the liberation of the holy city of Mecca. However, the relatively close Medina – the second holiest site of Islam, and some 380km further north – was left in Ottoman hands for the rest of the Great War. There were multiple reasons for this. The first, as noted, was that Sharif Hussein never had the reported 30,000 warriors under control, while the Ottoman garrison was about 20,000 strong (mostly from the 22nd Division, headquartered in Hejaz; in turn the 22nd was subordinated to the VII Corps, headquartered in Yemen). Indeed, although in receipt of so much funding from London (something like ten times more than ibn Saud), and therefore capable of equipping and controlling several armies, Sharif Hussein was not even in control of more than 30% of the Arabian Peninsula and its population. Contrary to British expectations (as well as the plentiful urban legends and wishful thinking regularly circulated ever since), not only did the

Sharif Hussein ibn Ali, who led the 'Arab Revolt' from Mecca in June 1916 in a bold move. He launched the uprising without British commitment or support, in an attempt to force London (and thus Paris, too) into accepting him as the ruler of 'all Arabs'. (Tom Cooper collection)

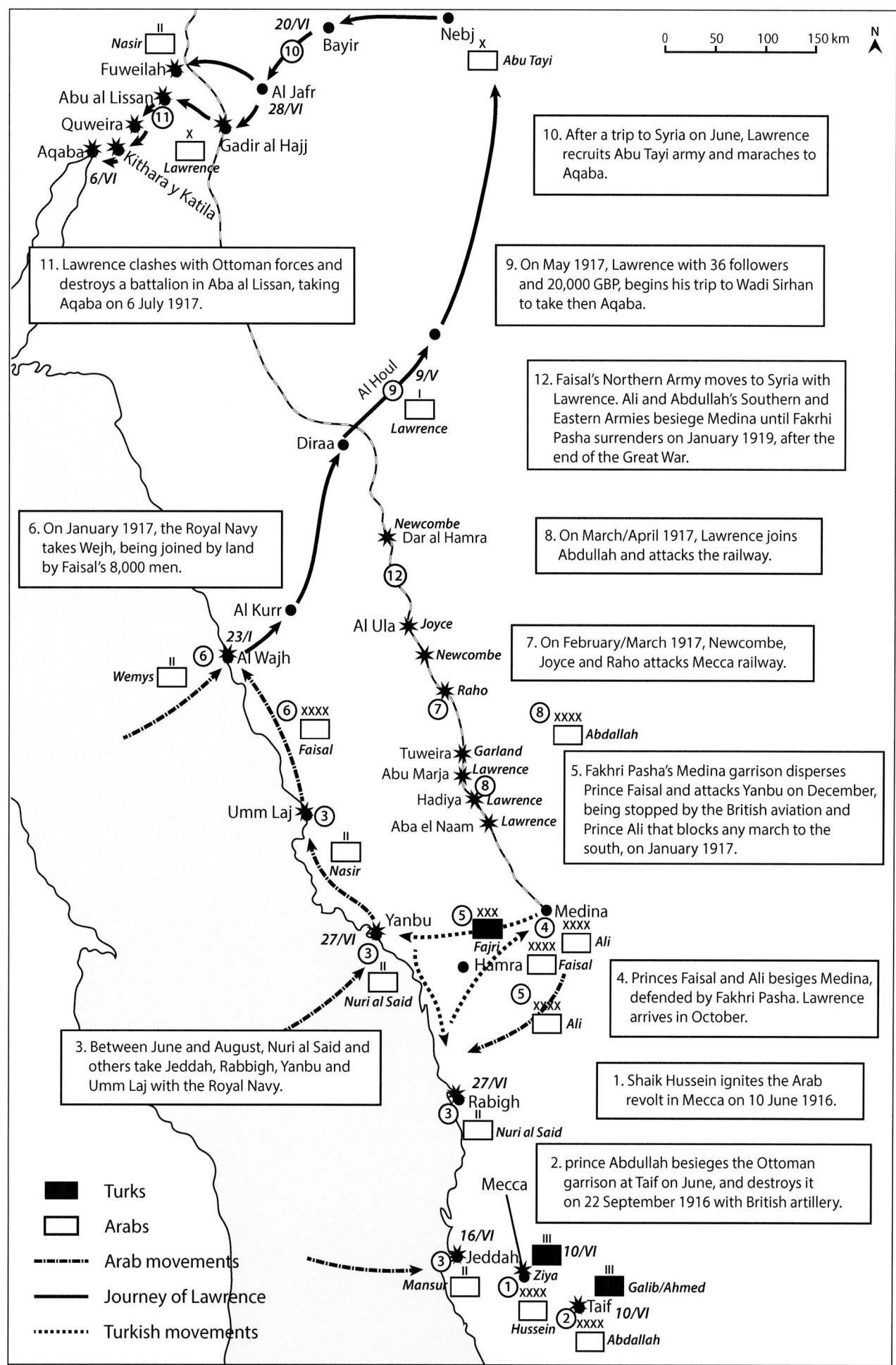

A map of the main locations of the Arab Revolt in Hejaz. (Map by George Anderson based on Desperta Ferro and de Gabiola)

mass of Arabs remained outside the Hashemite reach, the mass of Arab officers and other ranks serving in the Ottoman Army fiercely resisted all the British offers to defect and join Hussein. Similar was true for the majority of civilian Arab nationalists living in the Ottoman Empire.[5]

Unsurprisingly, precisely because they were facing so much resistance in the Arab world, the British not only took care to present Sharif Hussein as the head of the Arab world – although they knew he had no power base outside Hejaz – but subsequently appointed three of his sons as monarchs of four different countries. Three of these were artificial by nature and carved out by administrators from London. Ali ibn Hussein would succeed his father as the King of Hejaz; Abdullah would end up being the King of Transjordan, while Faisal first dared declare himself the King of the Arab Kingdom of Syria (where he, following the Armistice of Mudros which officially ended the First World War in the Middle East, did attract attention and support of at least some of Arab officers of the Ottoman Army), before being expelled by the French, and then enthroned by the British as the King of Iraq.

As of 1916, however, that was all still the future. Thus, it was particularly surprising – especially for ibn Saud – when, in October 1916, Sharif Hussein publicly announced that the British had recognised him as the 'King of Arabs'.

SECURING MECCA AND JEDDAH

Mecca was defended by about 1,500 Ottoman soldiers grouped in the, so-called, *Mekke Kumandani*, or Mecca Command, commanded by Major Ziya. This contingent included two battalions of the 22nd Division (the III of the 128th Regiment, and the II of the 130th Regiment), a company of former Sudanese slaves, two mountain batteries with seven or eight guns, a Gendarmerie detachment, and a Support Company. As of June 1916, most of these units were much weakened, because their officers and other ranks were on leave in the much cooler Ta'if for a summer vacation. Moreover, their bases in the Mecca area were scattered between the Governor's Office, the main barracks and the fortress of Jiyad.

Table 9: Ottoman Army, Mecca Command (Major Ziya), June 1916

Unit	Notes
III Battalion, 128th Regiment	from 22nd Division
II Battalion, 130th Regiment	from 22nd Division
Sudanese Company	
Support Company	
2 mountain batteries	7-8 guns
Gendarmerie (detachment)	
Total: 1,500 troops	

Sharif Hussein's shot in the air was a signal for his followers to attack the Ottomans, provoking multiple fire-fights. However, by the following morning his warriors had only managed to overpower the Governor's Office. The main barracks and the fortress of Khiyad remained under the Ottoman control – to no small degree because the troops there were supported by machine guns and artillery. Now both sides settled down to wait for reinforcements: the Hashemites for further deliveries of arms, ammunition and money from the British, and the Ottomans for a relief force from Medina. However, in July 1916, the British sent one infantry battalion and an artillery battery of the Egyptian Army via the Red Sea. Their bombardment forced the garrison of the Jiyad fortress to capitulate. The artillery was then lined-up in front of the barracks and opened fire, setting them alight. By 9 July, the last Ottoman garrison in Mecca had suffered around 300 killed, and was left without option but to capitulate. The Hashemites secured about 8,000 Ottoman rifles, along with five cannons.

A few weeks earlier, on 5 June, Amir Abdullah, the son of the Sharif who with his diplomatic skills had begun to win over the British, approached Taif, east of Mecca. He led some 5,000 warriors, under the guise of 'pursuing pro-British Arabs'. With telegraph communications to Mecca cut off since 10 July, the Governor and commander of the 22nd Division, Ghalib Pasha, suspected nothing. Then, at sunset that day the Arabs attacked the north side of the city. The garrison, commanded by Ahmed Bey, was a potent force, however, including some 3,000 officers and other ranks of the I and III Battalions, 129th Regiment, 22nd Division. They were also

The Holy City of Mecca, where the Arab Revolt began. (Abd al-Ghaffar, As-Sayyid, US Library of Congress)

SWORDS OF SAUD VOLUME 1: THE BIRTH OF A DESERT EMPIRE 1902-1921

A reconstruction of Saud's successful assault on Riyadh, in 1902. *As the sun rose, Saud* (right) *listens to the noise of the heavy gates of the Mismak opening and there he sees Ajlan* (the Rashidi governor, his enemy) *coming out with an escort of six men still sleepy but armed with swords. The Prince did not hold back, and in a fit of fury he shouted: "I will kill you, come on, akhu Nura!" (I am Nura's brother). Saud goes downstairs and charges at Ajlan, followed by his warriors. Ajlan* (left) *struggles to get rid of his blue padded winter cloak with red edges, and gives Saud a sword hit from above, that he is able to barely stop with his musket.* (Artwork by Renato Dalmaso)

The reconstruction to the left shows a young Ibn Saud, as of around 1902. His robe is typical for his tribe, and including the red and white *Keffiyeh* on his head, and an *Agal* (black rope with knots) to hold it in place, a white *Thobe* (long white gown), and a *Bisht* (a brown, camel-hair cloak edged in gold) on the top. He is shown as armed with a long, ceremonial, hunting musket, as on display in the al-Masmak Museum in Riyadh, and a dagger. The reconstruction to the right shows a young Ibn Rashid, one of Saud's major rivals. Both his Keffiyeh and his Agal were much more colourful than the austere models worn by the Sauds. While also wearing a white Thobe, this was covered by a dark *Bisht* made of fabric. (Artworks by Renato Dalmaso)

An Ikhwan warrior as seen around 1923. Notable are his short beard and a typical, open, white and plain turban. Underneath the same, he is shown wearing the *Keffiyeh* (the red-pattern drawn on the white cloth, typical for different Arab tribes). Characteristically, his robe is short, clearly showing the boots – as also typical for the Ikhwan. His armament included a Mauser rifle, a large knife with richly decorated scabbard, and a long sword. (Artwork by Renato Dalmaso)

SWORDS OF SAUD VOLUME 1: THE BIRTH OF A DESERT EMPIRE 1902-1921

A camel-mounted Saud warrior with the green flag (with white hoist and Qoranic verses) as photographed by Captain Shakespear in Thaji, in 1911. Camels were used for transportation but not for charging into battle, nor even for firing rifles at the enemy (except in an emergency, of course). Instead, most of the fighting took place on foot, with camel-mounted troops serving as an Arab version of Dragoons. (Artwork by Renato Dalmaso)

A Saudi warrior and standard-bearer (on foot) in typical, full-white dress reaching the ground, with an entirely white turban called a *Ghutrah*, and the *Agal* (black ropes with knots that held the turbans in place). Across his robes, he carries bandoliers with ammunition clips (either civilian or of Ottoman origin). His armament includes a long knife with a sober scabbard, and a British Martini rifle. The flag is as introduced in 1913, in Saud green and a white stripe on the hoist, with versicles from the Qoran. (Artwork by Renato Dalmaso)

This is a reconstruction of a member of the Hamidie Regiment, the Arab cavalry serving the Ottomans. They were equipped with (non-typical) bamboo lances, civilian bandoliers containing clips for their Mauser 1903 rifles, and long riding boots. Notable are the dark turban and robe, making this warrior easily distinguishable from those of the Sauds. (Artwork by Renato Dalmaso)

Top left: A typical infantryman of the Ottoman Army as of 1904: shown wearing the red *Fez* cap with blue tassel, and a dark blue uniform of the pattern M1893. More precisely, he is shown wearing only the blue shirt, but no blue jacket atop of it, because the latter was not necessary in the deserts of Arabia. His thick woollen leggings were tucked into socks, and he wore peasant shoes instead of boots. His firearm was a Mauser M1890, ammunition for which was carried in three bandoliers. (Artwork by Renato Dalmaso)

Top right: By 1914-1916, the pattern M1909 khaki uniform was in widespread service in the Ottoman Army. This corporal is shown wearing strap ranks on his shoulders (including a yellow bar on green), a mixture of civilian and Ottoman belts and bandoliers, and is armed with the Mauser M1890 rifle. (Artwork by Renato Dalmaso)

Right; Regular soldiers of the Hashemite Army of 1916-1920 (and then the Army of the Arab Kingdom of Syria) used to wear a mix of British and Ottoman uniform and gear. This one is shown as he would have been, for example, during the battle of Turaiba: wearing a Hashemite turban (which was often green; notably, the red and white Keffiyah typical for the Arab Legion seems to have been introduced several years later), British uniform, and Ottoman belt in leather. (Artwork by Renato Dalmaso)

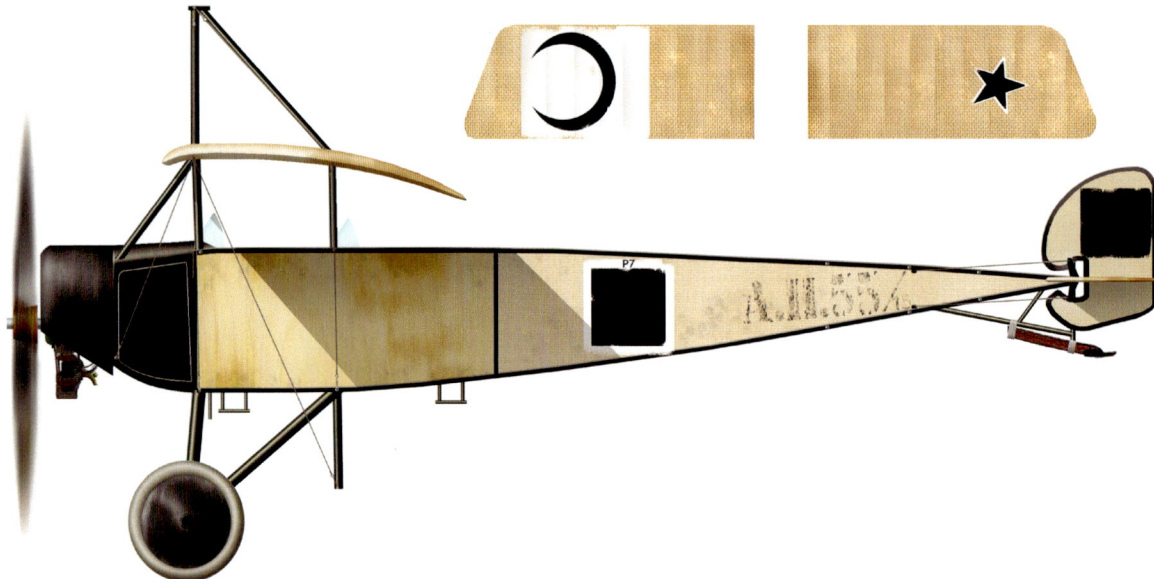

This is the reconstruction of the Pfalz A.II, marked as P7 – the former A.II.55 of the *Luftstreitkräfte* (air combat forces)– one of five to be deployed to Medina. Apparently left in canvas/fabric beige/plywood overall, the aircraft had the edges of the fuselage and struts painted in black. The engine cowling was in black as well. The Ottoman insignia was applied on the top of the wing (as shown in insert), the rear fuselage (together with the serial P7 on the white outline), and the fin. (Artwork by Tom Cooper)

This Rumpler C.Ia was perhaps the best known of German aircraft deployed with the Ottomans in the deserts of Arabia during the Great War: its original serial number was C.2627 (formerly 2627/16 of the Luftstreitkräfte's Pasha FA.33 in Palestine), but this was washed out from the fin. It received rather crudely applied Ottoman national insignia on the fuselage and the rudder. In 1917, a quote from the Qoran, Verse 13, known as as-Saff, was added to the national insignia applied on the fuselage, reading, 'Nusrun min Allah was Tathun Qaribun', or 'Help from God and speedy Victory'. (Artwork by Tom Cooper)

This is a reconstruction of the Albatross C.III marked as AK30 (applied in small black letters and digits within the white outline of the national marking on the fuselage). This aircraft had the construction number 599, and used to wear the serial number 2283-16, but this was badly worn out by the sun, sand, and (occasional) rain – as was its camouflage pattern, probably in dark or olive green and dark brown. (Artwork by Tom Cooper)

Manufactured starting in 1913, the Sopwith Schneider/Sopwith Tabloid seaplanes were famous for winning the Jack Schneider Cup Race of the following year. As of June-December 1916, a number were embarked on board the seaplane tenders *Ben-My-Chree* and *Raven II*. As far as is known, all were left in bare metal and canvas overall. This is the reconstruction of the aircraft that probably wore the tailfin number 3727, and was operated from *Raven II*. Together with other floatplanes, it was instrumental in seizing Jeddah and defending Yanbu. (Artwork by Luca Canossa)

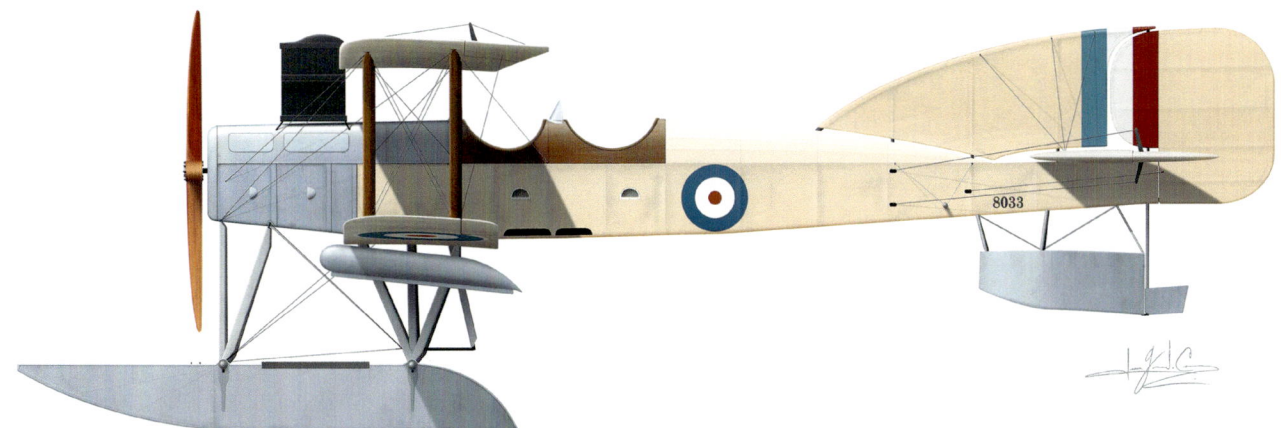

An even more important role during the fighting for Jeddah and Yanbu – but also at Gallipoli in 1915, Aden and several ports further north, before that point in time – was played by Short Type 184 amphibians: the type widely acknowledged as being the first to ever attack a ship with a torpedo. This example was embarked aboard the seaplane tender *Ben-My-Chree*, and should have worn the tailfin number 8033. (Artwork by Luca Canossa)

Although subsequently claiming a lot of fame for itself, due to the bad weather No. 14 Squadron of the Royal Flying Service only became operational late in the battle of Yanbu. For operations in the desert, the aircraft of this unit received colours as shown here, including the engine cowling in glossy black, wings and fin in canvas or linen colour, and the fuselage in brown (although some older colour profiles show their fins in brown, photographs are very clear in these being left in a lighter colour). The tailfin number of this example was 4483. (Artwork by Luca Canossa)

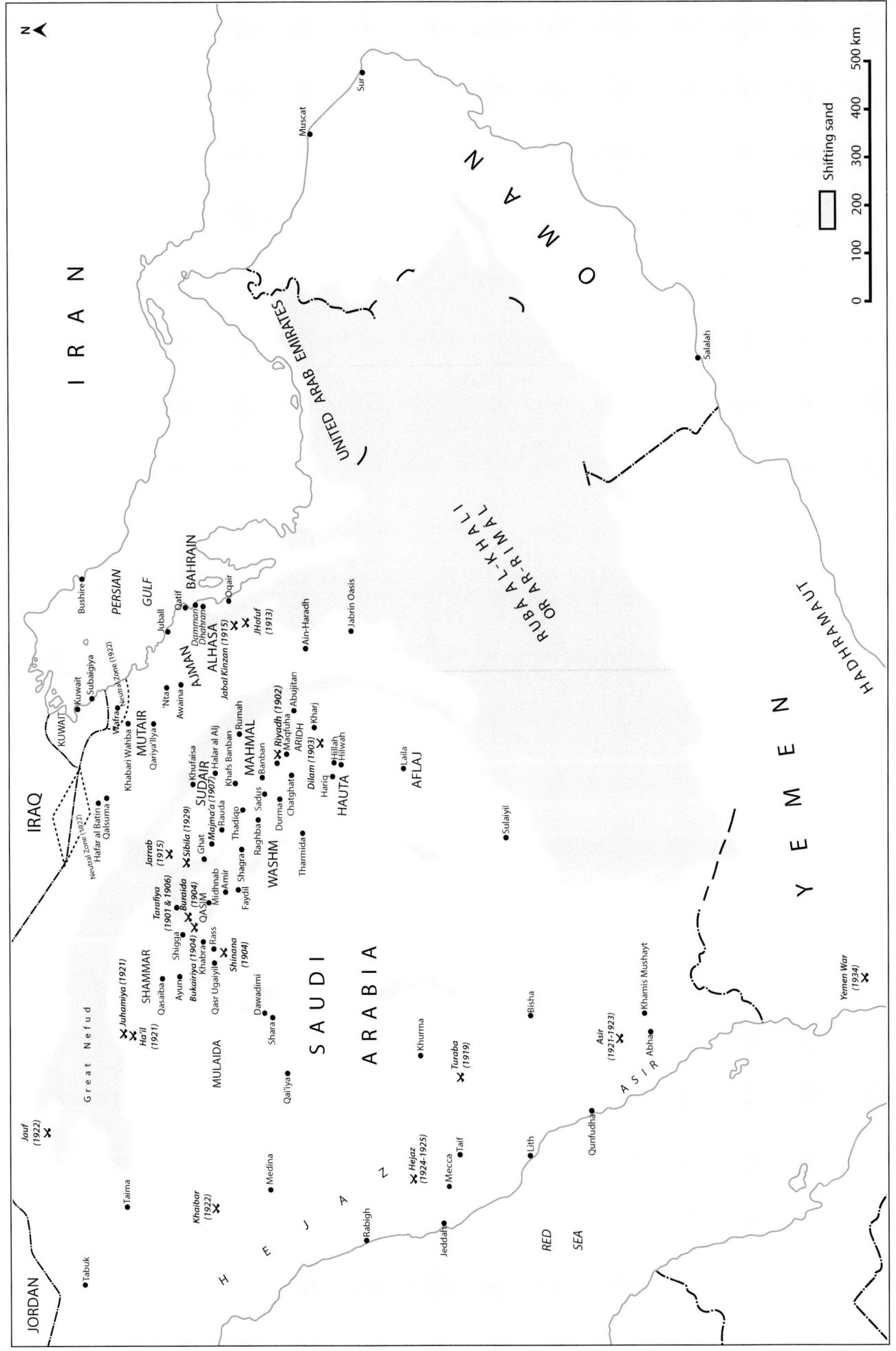

A map of the Arabian Peninsula with the major conquests by Ibn Saud of the period 1902-1925. Note: a rough outline of borders of the countries like Jordan, Iraq, United Arab Emirates, Oman and Yemen were added for orientation purposes: as of 1925, only Oman existed as such. Similarly, Iran was known as Persia until 1935. (Map by George Anderson based on Sander and de Gabiola)

A street view of the main street of Mecca during the 1920s, with the wall of the Great Mosque to the right. The street fighting initiated by the Hashemites ended with the surrender of the Ottoman governor's office. (Popperfoto, via Almana)

reinforced by a battalion of Gendarmerie, and two batteries of mountain artillery. Unsurprisingly, the Ottomans contained the attacks for several days, in similar fashion as in Mecca, forcing Abdullah's warriors to limit themselves to a blockade of the city until the arrival of artillery. The same Egyptian battery that forced the surrender at Mecca then reached Taif, but even so, it was not until 22 September that Ghalib Pasha gave up.

Table 10: Ottoman Army, Taif Garrison (Galib Pasha & Ahmed Bey), June 1916

Unit	Notes
Divisional Headquarters	from 22nd Division
I Battalion, 129th Regiment	from 22nd Division
III Battalion, 129th Regiment	from 22nd Division
Gendarmerie Battalion	
2 mountain batteries	
Total: 3,000 troops	

Meanwhile, further north, two other sons of the Sharif, Ali and Faisal, approached Medina with their own armies. Nominally at least, the local garrison was up to 10,000 strong. Actually, its commander, Fakhreddin or Fakhri Pasha, had about 6,400 under arms – including troops of the 22nd Division and the Hejaz Expeditionary Force, adding four battalions, two Cavalry, one Camel regiment, and five artillery batteries, and Gendarmerie. It was also connected to Damascus by the German-constructed railway. Unsurprisingly, Ali and Faisal initially focused on interdicting the railway traffic, which they began attacking on 8 June, actually before the official beginning of the uprising, with the intention of isolating Medina. However, Fakhri reacted by making an aggressive sortie out to meet them, and hit both from the rear so hard that their survivors dispersed. Leaving the majority of their troops behind, to continue investing Medina, Ali and Faisal then fled to the south. They returned to blockade Medina a few days later, but also kept their distance, always on alert for another possible raid by Fakhri.

Table 11: Ottoman Army, Medina Garrison (Fakhri Pasha), June 1916

Units & Sub-Units	Notes
Fort Medina Command	Badri Pasha
II Battalion, 129th Regiment	from 22nd Division
IV Battalion, 131st Regiment	from 22nd Division
Gendarmerie Battalion	
Railway Battalion	
2nd Akinci Arab Cavalry Regiment	
2 artillery batteries	
Hejaz Expeditionary Force	Fakhri Pasha
1st Akinci Arab Cavalry Regiment	
Hecins var Regiment	mounted on camels
3 artillery batteries	
2 signals companies	
Total: 10,000 troops	6,400 combatants
Reinforcements	arriving 28 October 1916

58th Division	Ali Necib
42nd Regiment	
55th Regiment	
130th Regiment	
Ester Infantry Battalion	mounted on mules
Mountain Artillery Battery	
in southern Vilayet Syria	
1st Provisional Force	Mehmed Cemal Pasha (Küçuk or Uçüncü), in Vilayet of Syria
138th Regiment	
161st Regiment	
I Battalion, 79th Regiment	
Gendarmerie Battalion of Ma´am	
2 companies from 31st and 130th Regiments	
2 railway companies	
3 cavalry squadrons	
Circassian Cavalry Regiment	
1 battery of 6th Field Artillery Battalion	

Ottoman General Fakhreddin Pasha, competent defender of Medina between 1916 to January 1919, and a hero for the Ottomans. (via *Desperta Ferro*)

Nuri al-Said, from Baghdad, was captured by the British while serving as an officer of the Ottoman Army. One of few the British managed to convince to join Hussein; he went on to command the 'regulars' of the Arab Army and took part in fighting for Rabegh and Yanbu before leading his troops with Lawrence and Faisal all the way to Damascus. Notable is his Hashemite *turban* with a British uniform, typical of the Arab Army and the subsequent Arab Legion, too. (*Desperta Ferro*)

At the same time, the rebellion was spreading along the coast, which was vital if the help of the British was to be obtained. Sheikh Mushin Mansur's forces attacked Jeddah. The garrison, under Major Hussein Husn, was about 2,000 strong, consisting of two battalions of the 22nd Division (the 1st and 2nd of the 128th Regiment), a Machine Gun Company (four guns) and an artillery battery (four guns). The Ottoman garrison repulsed the opening attack, on 9 June 1916, and then withstood five-days bombardment from the guns of Captain Boyle's Red Sea Patrol. However, on 15 June three seaplanes newly arrived from Aden aboard the tender HMS *Ben-My-Chree* appeared nearby. Commander C. R. Samson – captain of the tender and commander of the embarked aircraft – and Lieutenant Wedwood-Benn, his observer, made the first flight over Jeddah to photograph the defences and bomb artillery positions. Then they turned around and made a strafing run, deploying their Lewis machine gun. Initially, the Ottomans returned fire and both the aircraft and its pilot were hit: the propeller was damaged, causing severe vibrations, while Samson had a heel of his shoe shot off. However, the next two air strikes turned out to be too much for the garrison. First, a Sopwith 'Schneiders' attempted to breach the

Staff of Ottoman General Fakhreddin Pasha in the defence of Medina. (Bulent Yilmazer, via Uyar & Ericksson)

city wall using bombs of a 65lb (30kg) calibre, and then another dove to just 100ft (30.5 metres) to bomb and strafe with machine guns. At dawn of 16 June, as the HMS *Ben-My-Chree* was preparing its next series of air strikes, white flags appeared over Jeddah: the Ottoman garrison surrendered. Commander Samson later wrote: 'There is no doubt that three inefficient and rather antique seaplanes took Jeddah.'

With this port as a solid naval base from which the British could tranship their aid in larger amounts, the first regular elements of the Hashemite Army began to emerge. At the end of June, 700 Ottoman prisoners of war of Arab origin arrived (most were from territories of modern-day Iraq), they had been convinced to fight against the Ottomans. The Arab Regular Army had just been born. Under the command of Nuri al-Said, a former Ottoman officer in the service of the Hashemites, and with support from the Royal Navy, on 27 June the Arab regulars took the port of Rabigh (or Rabegh). Indeed, on the same day, they took Yanbu, further north, which was being defended by elements of the 45th and 129th Regiments. In August, the forces of as-Saad then secured al-Lith and Qunfudhah (which was already in Asir), to the south, and on the 15th, a force commanded by Nasir ibn Ali took Umm Lajj.[6]

Table 12: Ottoman Army, Jeddah Garrison (Major Husn), June 1916

Units & Sub-Units	Notes
I Battalion, 128th Regiment	from 22nd Division
II Battalion, 128th Regiment	from 22nd Division
Machine Gun Company	
Artillery Battery	

THE ARAB AND OTTOMAN DEPLOYMENT

Throughout July and August, the British turned Jeddah into a fortified naval base under the command of Colonel Cyril Wilson, and Allied aid began to flow with the arrival of 4,000 rifles, a battery of 4.5in howitzers, four mountain guns, eight machine guns and British uniforms. All this equipment made the regulars of Hussein's forces swell. Indeed, these were organised into the Arab Army, which was put under the command of Aziz Ali-al Masri, another former Ottoman officer and the founder of the regular Hashemite forces. These would reinforce the tribal contingents of the Royal Princes, becoming the nucleus of their forces, especially from mid-1917.

Meanwhile, the British and French Missions were strengthened: the latter, under the Lieutenant-Colonel Edoaurd Brémond, would focus on Mecca; and the former, instead, would do so through an unknown and extravagant intelligence officer named Thomas Edward Lawrence. Lawrence met with the different Hashemite Princes, and knew how to gain the trust of the mystic Faisal, whom he recommended to London as the best ally that the Empire could count on. Thus, Faisal was the one who began to receive the greatest amount of British aid, separating his force from those of his brother Ali. By the end of the year, what would be the Army of the North was west of Medina, on the coast, in Yanbu. Although still very scant, it would soon begin to contain regular army elements. The other armies would be those of the South, under Prince Ali, who was left guarding Medina; and that of the East, under Abdullah, who remained near Mecca, watching over the Rashidi of Shammar, pro-Ottomans, and the Saudis, their potential enemies. Abdullah counted from 16 October on the French support of eight sections of Hotchkiss machine guns, a battery of six mountain guns and another of field artillery, also of six pieces, a Company of Engineers, and another of support. In total, each of the three Hashemite armies would be of around 5,000 warriors.

The Ottomans reinforced their garrison at Medina via the railway too, however, and sent troops to Ma'an, Amman, and Damascus. On 28 October 1916, the 58th Division (including the 42nd, 55th, and 130th Regiments; Esters infantry battalion mounted on mules, and a battery of mountain artillery) arrived in Medina, commanded by Lieutenant-Colonel Ali Necib. The 1st Provisional Force followed, commanded by General Mehmed Cemal Pasha (also known as Küçuk or Uçüncü). It included the 138th and 161st Regiments, the I Battalion of the 79th Regiment, the Ma'an Gendarmerie Battalion, two companies drawn from the 31st and the 130th Regiments, two railway companies, three cavalry squadrons, a Circassian Cavalry Regiment, and a battery of the VI Battalion Field Artillery – and was deployed to protect the railway from Ma'an to Medina. In grand total, and together with the garrison of Medina, Fakhri Pasha thus had 12 battalions with 12,000 troops (of which about 9,000 were combat troops). These, as of 1 December 1916, were organised into three ad-hoc brigades.[7]

The future first King of Transjordan, Prince Abdullah ibn Ali of the Hashemites (seated), as seen in October 1916. Visible behind him and from left to right are Said Bey (another former Ottoman Army officer), Colonel Cyril Wilson, Aziz al-Masri (founder and supreme commander of the Arab Army), and Ronald Storrs. (via Murphy)

A machine gun section of the Ottoman Army in open position and ready for action. (US Library of Congress)

OTTOMAN AVIATION

An entirely new factor in the Arabian Peninsula appeared on 23 June 1916, when three German-made Pfalz A.IIs of the 3rd Bolük (squadron), commanded by Captain Cemil, departed for Medina. Two additional Pfalzs followed on 3 July. Cemal was temporarily deaf because he failed to wear a special helmet protecting his ears during a sandstorm. The deployment was carefully prepared. All pilots and mechanics had to be Muslims, and while originally wearing the initial Ottoman insignia – introduced in 1915, and consisting of a black square (usually covering the German black cross) – for operations in the holiest area of Islam, several aircraft had received red squares with a rising white moon instead. Three of Cemal's aircraft were delayed, however: they were held up in Syria by order of the commander of the IV Army. One of them was destroyed in an accident (possibly P8), which is why only four Pfalzs (P6, P7, P9, and P10), commanded by Lieutenants Fâzil and Sakir actually reached Medina, and then only between late August and 10 September 1916. By then, at least an airfield had been constructed, about six kilometres outside the city.

Throughout the autumn of 1916, the Ottoman airmen were primarily busy flying reconnaissance along the railway link from Medina to Ma'an. However, gradually, they began carrying light bombs and flew air strikes on any groups of Bedouins they found in the vicinity. For unknown reasons, not a single flight by the Pfalz P6 was ever recorded, indicating this became unserviceable soon after reaching Medina. This was unsurprising considering the difficulties of operating contemporary aircraft under desert conditions at the time. Because of the immense heat, taking off later than 20 minutes after dawn was extremely difficult, even hazardous. The hot and rarefied air made climbing extremely problematic, and the heat at altitudes above 500 metres unbearable. Even if the aircraft took off on time, it often took up to one hour to reach an altitude of a mere 950 metres. This in turn was insufficient to cross the mountains and run reconnaissance of the interior. Sudden changes in altitude were near-impossible, which is why not only air combat, but even ground attacks were de-facto impossible. Finally, locating rapidly moving Bedouin formations also proved extremely difficult, because these were always on the move and if stopped, then camped in tents that were earthy in colour, and thus almost perfectly camouflaged.

Table 13: 3rd Bolük, Ottoman Aviation in Hejaz, 1916-1917

Aircraft Type	Serial Number	Arrival	Notes
Pfalz A.II	P6	Jun/Jul 1916	no sorties recorded; probably cannibalised
Pfalz A.II	P7	Jun/Jul 1916	stored Jan 1917, probably destroyed in accident, Mar 1917
Pfalz A.II	P8	Jun/Jul 1916	destroyed in accident, Aug 1917
Pfalz A.II	P9	Jun/Jul 1916	retired in Jan 1917
Pfalz A.II	P10	Jun/Jul 1916	retired in Jan 1917
Albatross C.III	AK28	Nov 1916	destroyed in accident
Albatross C.III	AK30	Dec 1916	remained in Medina
Albatross C.III	AK31	Jan 1917	withdrawn to Vilayet Syria, mid-1917
Rumpler C.I	R2627	1917	periodically in Medina

Ottoman pilot Ibrahim Orhan, in front of his Pfalz A.II of the 3rd Bolük, before being sent to Medina. (Dr. David Nicolle collection)

The first combat experience for Ottoman fliers on the Arabian Peninsula took place on 27 October 1916. The Pfalz P7, piloted by Lieutenant Fâzil was fired upon by members of the Arab Army's mountain artillery battery deployed in the Bir ad-Dirwi area, close to Hadidah, while scouting the railway. It is very likely that the fire was ordered and directed by General al-Masry, an Egyptian advisor who served with Hussein's forces. He already had combat experience from Libya, which included fighting Italian-operated aircraft. Lieutenant Fâzil and his aircraft came away without any damage. Indeed, on the next day, he flew the same P7 all the way to the Red Sea, and scouted the coast for 2-and-a-half hours. However, after such a long mission, the Pfazl began losing power and altitude. Fâzil returned to Medina, and had the engine of his aircraft replaced twice – but without any effect. The conclusion was drawn: this was the wrong type of aircraft for operations in the Arabian skies. Therefore, Lieutenant Fâzil was sent back to Vilayet Syria to request deliveries of more powerful and more resilient aircraft. Two Albatross C.IIIs of the German 300th Bolük were sent by train for this purpose: AK28 (ex-2282/16), and AK30 (ex-2285/16). Both were operated by Ottoman pilots and assigned to the 3rd Bolük in Medina.

In early November 1916, the Ottoman airfield was moved to Bir-al-Abbas, recently recaptured by Fakhri's troops. From there, several sorties against Faisal's army were undertaken by Pfalz P7 and P10, by Lieutenants Fâzil and Sakir: Lawrence subsequently reported that their operations left the Arab regulars, undergoing training by el-Masry in Rabigh, demoralised.

Throughout that period, a small detachment of the 3rd Bölük, commanded by Lieutenant Saim, remained in Medina. The first Albatross finally arrived in Medina in late November. However, on the 26th of the same month, it was caught by a gust of wind while descending to 150 metres altitude in preparation to land. Surprised, Captain Saim miss-controlled the aircraft and crashed, dying in the accident. With this, the Ottoman detachment was reduced to the Pfalzs P7 and P10: once again, no operations by P6 and P9 were recorded, indicating both were out of commission and probably used as sources of spares or were being repaired.

The British reacted as well. On 14 October, at the insistence of Lawrence, Hussein, and also Lawrence's Oxford mentor, the archaeologist David Hogarth (acting Director of the Arab Bureau, an intelligence group in Cairo coordinating British support for Hussein), the order was issued for the deployment of C Flight of the No. 14 Squadron, Royal Flying Corps (RFC) to Rabegh. To highlight the significance of this decision, one should keep in mind that at the time the RFC had only 16 operational aircraft in all of Egypt, while the German Rumplers and Fokkers ruled the skies over the frontlines in the Sinai. However, the British understood the value of the aircraft so much that, in September, they organised the seaplane tender HMS *Anne* to sortie its two aircraft over Yanbu and Rabegh, 'to impress the Arabs'.

C Flight sailed for Rabegh on 14 October 1916 and reached its destination two days later. However, its landing was recalled when the Hashemite garrison in the port denied it the right to land, and General Reginald Wingate realised that the crews and their British infantry escort could offend religious sensitivity. Both Faisal and Lawrence insisted this was pushing religious sensitivities too far.

Capt Yüzbasi Saim, who flew the first Albatross to Medina, on 26 November 1916, only to be killed in an accident that also destroyed the airplane. (Dr. David Nicolle Collection)

A photo before the disaster: visible in the background, centre, is the Albatross AK 28, before being destroyed in Saim's accident, on 26 November 1916, in Medina. Visible to the right is a parasol Pfalz A.II wearing non-standard markings behind the wing: a black (or red) crescent and a star instead of a black square. In front of these devices, are the following pilots: Lieutenant Orhan (third from left); Lieutenant Rifat (sixth from right); and Captain Saim (extreme right), The photograph was taken just before the latter was killed. (Ole Nikolajsen Archive, via Dr. David Nicolle)

Indeed, Faisal's need for the aircraft meant he pressed the British for their troops and aircraft arrival in Rabegh. Thus, C Flight set sail again (this time under the command of Major A. J. Ross, who was fluent in Arabic) and landed from the merchant *El Kahira* at Rabegh on 16 November, accompanied by two Egyptian infantry companies, and four Rolls-Royce armoured cars. The disembarking of the aircraft took a combined effort by sailors of the guard ship, HMS *Minerva*, Joyce's Egyptian infantrymen, and the airmen – and included constructing a jetty, a road from the jetty to the local (recently constructed) aerodrome, the assembly of hangars and repair facilities, as well as the actual movement of the aircraft.

The unit thus arrived in the Arabian Peninsula including pilots Ross, Henderson, Bevan, Floyer, and Fordham, and four Royal Factory B.E.2 fighters (serial numbers 4478, 4483, 4488, and 5421), and became the core of the Hejaz Expeditionary Force. The first two sorties were flown on 24 November. Four days later, the four machines were flying photoreconnaissance of the surrounding area to enable creation of precise mapping of the challenging terrain. The defence of the port was in the hands of 500 Egyptian troops commanded by Major Joyce, while the wider territory around Rabegh was controlled by Prince Ali's Southern Army.[8]

Table 14: British Aviation in Hejaz, 1916-1917[9]

Aircraft Type	Serial Number	Arrival	Notes
East Indies and Egypt Seaplane Squadron, Royal Naval Air Service (Royal Navy)			
HMS Ben-My-Chree		Jun 1916	CO Commander Charles R. Samson
Short Type 184			
Short Type 184			
Sopwith Schneider	3772		
Sopwith Schneider	3773		
Sopwith Schneider	3774		
Sopwith Schneider	3775		
HMS Raven II		Dec 1916 – Jan 1917	
Sopwith Schneider	3727		
Sopwith Schneider	3777		
Sopwith Schneider	3778		
Sopwith Schneider	3790		
C Flight, No. 14 Squadron, Royal Flying Corps			CO Major A. J. Ross
B.E.2	4478	Nov 1916 – Jul 1917	
B.E.2	4483	Nov 1916 – Jul 1917	
B.E.2	4488	Nov 1916 – Jul 1917	
B.E.2	5421	Nov 1916 – Jul 1917	

FAKHRI'S COUNTEROFFENSIVE

With his reinforced formations in place, Fakhri made the next move – the urgency for which was made obvious on 24 November, when an RFC aircraft operating from Egypt attacked the Hejaz railway north of Ma'an, dropping delayed fuse, 100 pound bombs into railway culverts from an altitude of a mere 20 feet.[10] On 1 December 1916, he sortied in a western direction with two of his three brigades (around 6,000 troops in total). The Pfalz P7 piloted by Lieutenant Fâzil flew reconnaissance ahead and by 4 December, the pilot delivered several self-drawn maps of the area. On the ground, the Ottomans first dodged the Bani Salem tribe that was watching them from Wadi Safra, west of Medina. Prince Ali, who was on the coast near Rabegh, then sent his brother Emir Sayd to prevent the Ottomans from reaching Hamra. However, Fakhri's troops easily swept beside this attempt and continued their advance. Further north, Faisal was in Yanbu and advancing on Nakhl Mubeirik with about 4,000 warriors, and thus mistakenly had left his naval base undefended. Therefore, it was on the British fliers to locate the approaching Ottoman force. Lawrence complained that the RFC aerial activity was unsatisfactory – at least in contrast to the 'yeoman work' of the seaplanes from HMS *Raven II*. The actual problem was a combination of bad weather that had grounded B.E.2s of C Flight, and the short range of its aircraft. So, who exactly detected the approach of Fakhri's force thus remains unclear. According to one version, on 8 December, one of the B.E.2s spotted the Ottomans in the Bir Said area, while operating at the limit of its range (indeed, so much, the aircraft had to land at Yanbu to refuel, before returning to Rabegh). However, British historians point out that C Flight was still grounded and that instead it was a pair of the Royal Navy's Short Type 184 and/or Sopwith Schneider seaplanes from the HMS *Raven II*, who detected the three Ottoman brigades advancing from Medina towards Yanbu, on 10 December – and also had to report that the Sharifian covering force of 1,500 all but disappeared.[11]

By then, Fakhri had divided his force into three groups. One went after Faisal, dispersing his Northern Army in a series of clashes between 3 and 9 December, before continuing for Yanbu. In relation to this activity, on 9 December, the Pfalz P7 piloted by Lieutenant Fâzil flew reconnaissance to monitor the Ottoman rear, in the Medina direction, to make sure the Arabs were not trying to fall on the reduced garrison.

The second of Fakhri's groups went straight for Yanbu, where Major Garland had gathered 1,500 Arab warriors for the defence – before, as mentioned above, they dispersed. Fortunately for the British, Joyce could count on five warships of the Royal Navy's Red Sea Patrol, including HMS *Dufferin*, monitor HMS *M31* (with two Mk.XII guns calibre 152mm), and the aircraft carrier HMS *Raven II*. The Short Type 184 and/or Sopwith Schneider seaplanes from the latter repeatedly attacked the enemy column using bombs and machine guns, eventually forcing it to stop during the night from 11 to 12 December 1916. As the weather improved, on 6 January 1917, C Flight flew its first air strike against the third Ottoman column, when three aircraft led by Ross bombed its camp at el-Hajah.

Meanwhile, on Lawrence's advice, Faisal's other armies rushed to attack the Ottoman supply links: in the Khaybar Oasis, Emir Abdullah's Eastern Army overpowered the Ottoman column commanded by Ashraf Bey. Farther southeast, it overran a convoy underway to Mecca, capturing GBP 20,000 in gold. On 14 December 1916, the Ottoman aircraft were deployed to find the enemy columns. Both Pfalzs P7 and P10 took off, but – probably concerned about the appearance of British aircraft – Lieutenants Fâzil and Sakir flew together, thus greatly decreasing the total area they could scout. To their aid came the more robust Albatross C.III serial number AK30. On 27 December, Lieutenant Fâzil flew it to reconnaissance and strike at the port of Yanbu, but thick fog forced him to abort the mission. By that date, the Pfalz P9 was back in operation, but Lieutenant Sakir failed to find the enemy. The same was valid for Fâzil's next reconnaissance mission: on 31 December, he made a flight in P9, but without success. Amid decreasing enthusiasm for continuous rebellion, Faisal's armies' disappeared in the desert. Uncertain about the reasons for his enemy's disappearance, Fakhri ended up becoming indecisive about what to do as next. He might have sensed imminent danger, but certainly did not expect the blow he was about to receive.

Major Garland, defender of Yanbo and saboteur of the Hejaz railway using mines he had invented; the devices became known as 'Garland Mines'. (via Murphy)

FAISAL´S COUNTERSTROKE

Although his rebellion was on the verge of collapsing, and a large part of his forces were scattered by the Ottoman advance on Yanbu, Faisal was not defeated. He managed to regroup about 1,200 Bedouin from the Agayl, Juhayna, Harb, and Billi tribes, and continued marching north along the coast, onto the Ottoman-controlled port of Wejh. Moreover, the defences of Yanbu were reinforced by Abdullah's Eastern Army, the bulk of which re-deployed from Mecca to Wadi 'Ais, in turn threatening the Medina railway. Thanks to British gold, additional tribes then began joining, bolstering Faisal's numbers to around 8,000: the largest Arab army in living memory of most of participants. Lawrence and Faisal were thus able to arrange a two-prong assault on Wejh: the main attack coming from the land, while 600 Arab regulars embarked on Admiral Rosslyn Wemyss' Red Sea Flotilla. The attack began with an amphibious landing directly inside the port, supported by artillery from HMS *Hardinge*, HMS *Fox*, and HMS *Espiegle*. The Ottoman garrison, consisting of the 129th Battalion with about 800 troops, and 600 camel-mounted Agayl, fought back for a day. However, on 23 January, it was informed about the approach of Faisal and Lawrence's ground forces, and quickly withdrew, constantly harassed by naval gunfire.

The loss of Wejh was a blow that the Ottoman Army strongly felt. Rather unsurprisingly, it reacted by dispatching additional aircraft to Medina, including four Albatrosses (AK4, AK31, AK40, and AK72) and three Rumpler C.Is (R1837, R1847, and R2627). While it remains unclear exactly how many of them had actually reached their new base, and at what point in time – apparently, several were held up by local commanders in the Amman area – it is known that in early 1917, the surviving three Pfalzs (P7, P9, and P10), were put into reserve, and only the last Albatross C.III (AK30) remained operational.

Yanbu camp, in January 1917, being defended in absence of his commander by Major Garland and the Royal Navy. (via Murphy)

An Albatross C.III after an unknown accident in Medina, luckily not a fatal one. Perhaps it was the AK30 after aborting the mission to Yanbu due to thick fog. Notable are the black squares on the wings and the tail. (Ole Nikolajsen Archive, via Nicolle)

The port of Wejh, taken by a landing party of the Arab Army before the arrival of Faisal. It would become the major base of the Northern Army for its attacks on the middle section of the Medina-Damascus railway, and then, for Faisal's advance on Aqaba. (Bailloud Collection, SHD Vincennes, via Murphy)

Hashemite Prince Faisal, commander of the Arab Northern Army, friend of Lawrence, who would conquer Damascus and declare himself the King of the Arab Kingdom of Syria, before – three years later – being enthroned the King of Iraq by the British. He was played by Alec Guinness in David Lean's mythical film *Lawrence of Arabia*. (Dr. David Nicolle collection))

Faisal's Northern Army, with Lawrence, both in the centre, departing from Yanbu to attack Wejh, in December 1916. (Dr. David Nicolle Collection)

Hashemite Prince Faisal with his Army of the North, *"the largest Arab Army in living memory"* marching to Wejh, in January 1917. (Casado, via Serga)

THE THIRD COLUMN IN THE SOUTHERN SECTOR

While all this was happening in the north, a third Ottoman column had marched south along the coast aiming to challenge and defeat Prince Ali and his Southern Army at Rabegh. While a highly-promising move early on, before long this effort became a demonstration of what can happen to an army exposed to air power in the desert. On 6 January 1917, three B.E.2s of C Flight attacked the column for the first time. Additional air strikes followed on 16 and 25 January, eventually forcing the Ottomans to stop in Derb as-Sultani, a mere 25 kilometres from their objective. By that point in time one of the new Ottoman Albatross C.IIIs – serial number AK31 – had become available. On 14 and 15 January, piloted by a newcomer pilot, Lieutenant Cevdet, this was deployed together with the Sakir-flown AK30 into reconnaissance and air strikes on Prince Ali's army in the south. Their activity was sufficient for the British to deploy their B.E.2s into combat air patrols over the Abbud area, on 29 January, aiming to intercept and shoot them down. However, the Ottoman aircraft did not re-appear. By this time, in light of losing Wejh, Fakhri had realised that the focal point of Faisal's offensive was in the north, that his forces were overstretched, and in danger of being isolated from their supply bases. Therefore, he ordered his third column back to Medina. The British were thus left free to convert Wejh into the main base of Faisal's Northern Army. Indeed, it was from here that the allies could plan an advance all the way to Aqaba, and then further north – in the direction of Jerusalem and Damascus – thus converting this campaign from an affair of tactical, into one of strategic importance.[12]

A B.E.2 of Flight C of the 14th British RFC Squadron, based at Wejh, with Captain Wilkinson and Lieutenant Henderson. These airplanes were vital in spoiling Fakhri Pasha's offensive against Rabegh. (Dr. David Niccolle Collection)

A detail-view of a B.E.2, probably with Lieutenant Murphy, in the Ma'an area in 1918. (IWM Q58702 via Murphy)

THE LEGEND OF LAWRENCE OF ARABIA

The Arab-British victory at Wejh came at the most opportune moment. It greatly raised spirits all over the British Empire – even more so considering General Archibald Murray's Egyptian Expeditionary Force (EEF) defeated the Ottomans in Romani, Magdhaba and Rafa, but was then defeated in the First- and Second Battles of Gaza. While busy firing Murray and finding a replacement for him, the War Office, aware that Faisal could not destroy the Ottomans in the Arabian Peninsula, instructed Lawrence to prevent Fakhri Pasha from sending reinforcements to the Sinai front by isolating Medina. For this purpose, Lawrence organised a series of systematic raids from Wejh against the central section of the railway. This was a long distance from Medina and thus hard to protect.

The raids went on into June and then July 1917, gradually cutting off the supply of ammunition for the Ottoman artillery in Medina. As was expected, the Ottomans deployed their few aircraft to search for raiding parties. However, their efforts were marred by constantly increasing problems. Not only were the remaining Pfalzs worn out and had to be limited in use as training tools, but in late March, Lieutenant Fâzil crashed the venerable P7, after about 150 hours of flying. Thereafter, Albatrosses took over, and flew numerous reconnaissance missions along the railway track. On 14 March, the British re-deployed B.E.2s of Flight C to Wejh (with a refuelling stop in Yanbu), and these greatly helped Lawrence's Arabs in continuing their raids, before being returned to Egypt on 30 July, to serve on the Sinai front.

Above: Second from the left, Colonel Stewart Newcombe; second from the right, Major al-Masri, and then Lieutenant Hornby, during one of several raids made to cut the Hejaz railway in July 1917. (Dr. David Nicolle Collection)

Left: The house of the British Mission at Wejh, with a Bedouin carrying a SMLE rifle at its entrance. This port would be the main British base until the taking of Aqaba. (Bailloud Collection, SHD, Vincennes, via Murphy)

Meanwhile, in Wejh, Faisal reorganised his forces. Tribes from the south began to leave and were largely replaced by tribes from the north – including several from the Vilayet Syria. The Juhayna left for their home in the Wadi Janbu, and men of the Howeitat, Shararat, Bani 'Atiya, and Rwalla replaced them. Among the Howeitat was Auda Abu Tayi, leader of the Abu Tayi clan of the Huwaitát. Not only was this man able to brag about the murder of several Ottoman tax collectors and boast about killing 75 people with his own hands, but his Bedouin proved fierce combatants, who convinced Lawrence to start acting on his own and to move to the outskirts of Ma'an, in today's Jordan. Contrary to instructions provided by Gilbert Clayton, who explicitly told Lawrence that a 'move to Aqaba on the part of Faisal is not at present desirable…' – because of the McMahon-Husayn Correspondence being superseded by the Sykes-Picot Treaty, Lawrence brought forward instead the decision to advance into the Vilayet Syria.

Obviously, such an undertaking – including the crossing of the Hejaz Mountains and the western side of the Nafud Desert with a large army, and then assaulting well-fortified Aqaba – was out of question. Without British support, Faisal lacked the necessary supplies, while it was also a move that would attract Ottoman attention. Therefore, Lawrence set out, guided by Sherif Nasir, and accompanied by Auda and only 21 other warriors, and GBP 20,000 in gold, with the aim to recruit Bedouins along the way and then assault Aqaba, deep behind the Ottoman frontlines. It was expected that this would collapse the Ottoman front in the Sinai and make the way free for an advance by the Arab Army in a northern direction. Indeed, it was expected to bring the Hashemties out of their isolation deep in the Hejaz, and to link them up with the British.

Lawrence and Abu Tayi, the stiking character played by Anthony Quinn in the film Lawrence of Arabia. It was Tayi who convinced Lawrence to attack the port of Aqaba – also because the area was close to the territory of his tribe, the Huwaitát. (IWM Q58707, via Murphy)

LAWRENCE TAKES AQABA

Lawrence and Auda Abu Tayi departed from Wejh on 9 May, starting one of most spectacular raids in the history of modern warfare, and which was to see them travel over 1,000 kilometres to achieve it. At first, they marched in a northeast direction, to cross the Medina-Ma'an railway in the Dira'a area. Then they crossed one of the most inhospitable deserts in the word – called *al-Houl* (The Terrible) by the local Arabs. From there, they continued along the Wadi Fejr, before turning northwest and marching for 200-300 kilometres along the Wadi Sirhan. Once they had reached the spring pastures in the Huwaitát territory, Tayi began using gold to recruit local warriors, while Lawrence continued for 800 kilometres further north, crossing the Syrian Desert to reach the outskirts of Damascus and inspire the revolt of the Metawila tribe. Surprised by the trouble deep in their rear, the Ottomans were forced to re-deploy six battalions from the front to quell the uprising.

Auda Abu Tayi with some of his Huwaitát. He bragged to have killed 75 people with his own hands; he then went on to take Aqaba, changing the course of the war in the Middle East. (IWM Q60169, via Murphy)

A picture taken by Lawrence of Faisal´s army charging to enter Aqaba. (Dr. David Nicolle collection)

By the time Lawrence returned to Wadi Sirhan, on 17 June 1917, Auda Abu Tayi had recruited about 500 Huwaitát, 160 Rwalla and Shararat, and 35 Kwakiba to his side. They set out to feint an attack on Damascus; seizing several forts, wells, and the railways near Amman and Dera'a along the way, and massacring enemy garrisons in the process. The Ottomans reacted by deploying a battalion from the 178th Regiment from Ma'an, and this recovered the Fort Fuweilah before proceeding toward Aba al-Lissan. However, on 2 July 1917, Auda Abu Tayi ambushed, surrounded and annihilated the Ottoman force after Lawrence incited his warriors by shouting, 'shoot a lot and hit a little'. Over 300 Ottoman troops were killed, and some 160 taken prisoners – though, this time, the latter were well treated.

Following this defeat, several Ottoman garrisons in the same area all surrendered without a fight, in turn encouraging additional Huwaitát and even some Haywat to bolster the raiding party to around 1,000. Emboldened, Lawrence and Auda Abu Tayi then went straight for Aqaba, and secured the crucial port without firing a shot: the garrison, including two companies of Gendarmerie and elements of the 161st Regiment, had abandoned the place shortly before their arrival. On 7 July 1917, Lawrence crossed the Sinai desert, and, 49 hours later, arrived to report in Cairo – still dressed in his worn-out Arab robes. Although the new commander of the Egyptian Expeditionary Force, General Edmund Allenby, was incredulous, eventually, he understood the importance of Lawrence's achievement. Henceforth, he gave free rein for additional shipments of supplies, arms, and ammunition to the Arab Army, aiming to enable it to provide direct support for the overall war effort.[13]

The mythical Lawrence of Arabia, who (together with Auda Abu Tayi) took Aqaba after a 1,000 kilometre long march in the desert, before (in attempt to spoil the Sykes-Picot Treaty) pushing Faisal's Arab Army all the way to Damascus, thus changing the course of the war in the region – and the history of the Middle East, too. (Lowell Thomas, Photo Aísa, via Desperta Ferro)

The port of Aqaba, nowadays the southernmost point in Jordan. After being taken by Lawrence, Faisal's Arab Army was brought there to continue attacking into the rear of the Ottoman deployment in the southern Vilayet Syria, thus greatly supporting Allenby's advance. (Dr. David Nicolle collection)

The port of Aqaba, with HMS *Humber*. (via Murphy)

FAISAL'S MOVE TO SYRIA

The next move, as was promised by Allenby to Lawrence, saw the British help ship a large portion of Faisal's Arab Army to Aqaba. The port was turned into a major depot of the Royal Navy, including a landing strip built at Kuntila. From there, by August 1917, the Royal Flying Corps bombed Ma'an, Abu al-Lissan and Fuweilah, further bolstering Arab raids against the Hejaz railway. Foremost, Aqaba became a major base of the Arab Army, which was then deployed to protect the eastern flank of the Egyptian Expeditionary Force's advance into Palestine. This action not only saw the Arab Army leave the environment of the Arabian Peninsula, but also saw it liberating a huge portion of territory all the way to Damascus, which it reached on 1 October 1918. Unsurprisingly, the Hashemites claimed this entire area for themselves. While this claim and the operations in question are beyond the scope of this book, they are important to keep in mind: foremost, because they brought the Hashemites on a collision course with both London and Paris, as they were threatening to ruin the Sykes-Picot arrangements. Furthermore, thanks to extensive British help, they were now the primary enemies of ibn Saud, and were in possession of – theoretically – a far superior armed force.

Throughout 1918, this Northern Army that had moved to the Vilayet of Syria was commanded by Faisal and consisted of about 8,000 combatants. Its second-in-command became Faisal's younger brother, Zaid ibn Hussein. About 2,000 of his troops were regular soldiers: initially commanded by el-Masri. They were primarily former soldiers of the Ottoman Army, mostly of Arab origin,

An exhausted Lawrence on his arrival in Damascus, in 1918. (IWM Q73534, via Murphy)

captured, convinced to switch sides, then re-trained by the British, and supplied with their uniforms, arms, equipment and gear. This was the only part of Faisal's force capable of fighting 'conventionally', or in the 'contemporary European style' – as proved during the battle of Ma'an, in April 1918.

The regulars were commanded by one of few captured officers of the Ottoman Army who agreed to join Faisal: Jaafar Pasha al-Askari. His chief-of-staff (and brother-in-law) was Nuri al-Said – who had excelled while conquering parts of the centre Hejaz in the summer of 1916.[14] Their force was organised into two small divisions, each of which actually resembled a regiment:

- The 1st, based in Aqaba, was commanded by Brigadier-General Amin al-Asil, and included two battalions of around 400 troops each;
- The 2nd, based in Quwayra, was commanded by Lieutenant-Colonel Majid Hasun, and also included two battalions.

Their supporting elements included two batteries with eight artillery pieces in all, operated by around 150 men; a machine gun detachment, a battalion of the Hejaz Camel Corps, and another of mule-mounted infantry.

Except for the regulars, the Arab Army also had a tribal component – the Huwaitát, the Bani Ali, the Bali, the Juhainah, and the 'Ataiba – and it included a contingent of the British Army. Within the framework of the Operation Hedgehog (The British military mission to aid the Arab Army), Colonel Pierce C. Joyce (replaced by Colonel Alan Dawney on 18 March 1918) led British, Egyptian, and Ghurka troops. These were organised into a 300-strong company of the Imperial Camel Corps, the Hejaz Company with Rolls-Royce armoured cars, and the Hejaz Battery of Talbot cars armed with 10-Pounder guns.

Jafar Pasha al-Askari, new commander of the Arab Army, on the left; then Prince Faysal, leader of the Northern Army; and finally, to the right, Colonel Pierce C. Joyce, commander of Operation Hedgehog (British forces in the Hejaz). Photo taken in August 1917. (via Murphy)

An Arab Army Talbot car at Wadi Ithm, with Faisal, and Abu Tayi behind the driver, in March 1918. (via Murphy)

MEDINA'S FATE

With Faisal's Arab Army driving far to the north, the Ottoman forces still in the Arabian Peninsula were growing isolated. It was no surprise, when Lieutenant Fâzil was ordered to withdraw the 3rd Bölük back to Ma'an: it was more important to deploy his troops against the Egyptian Expeditionary Force than to keep it at the isolated position in Medina, whose possession had been rendered useless for anything other than propaganda purposes. Indeed, even the train convoy carrying the aircraft out of the city had to break through and fight off several Arab raids on its way north. Once it reached Ma'an, only the Albatross serial number AK30 was left there. The Rumpler serial number R2627 bearing an inscription from the Qoran in its black rectangle, which probably comes from its time in Medina (the caption reads "*Help from God and a Speedy Victory*") – and its pilot, Lieutenant Orhan – were eventually both sent further north, and served the rest of the war in the Vilayet Syria.

A Rumpler C.I of the 3rd Boluk, as seen in Ma´an, in March 1918. By this time, the aircraft had been used to serve the defence of Medina and had received a Qoranic inscription on its black triangle, reading 'Help from God and a Speedy Victory'. (Dr. David Nicolle Collection)

The Ottoman Army, mainly made up of Arab soldiers (see their turbans) in a review by Jemal Pasha and Kress von Kressenstein in Jerusalem of December 1917. (US Library of Congress)

The remaining Ottoman Army positions in Hejaz were kept under pressure by the other two of Faisal's armies. The Prince Ali's Army of the South, around Medina, grew to around 9,000 and included a contingent of Arab regulars (comprising two battalions of infantry, one of mule-mounted infantry, one of camel-mounted infantry, four batteries of artillery, and a company of engineers), but mostly consisted of warriors from Arab tribes of the centre and southern Hejaz. Abdullah's Army of the East, who, on top of watching Medina, had an eye on the pro-Ottoman Rashidi of Shammar, and the Sauds, his potential enemies, comprised another 9,000, primarily from tribal contingents, but which also included a 'regular' element in the form of two camel-mounted battalions, a cavalry squadron, and a battery of mountain artillery. Starting in March 1917, these two Corps were supported by a French Military Mission. This included 47 officers and 1,127 other ranks, organised into a Mixed Cavalry Marching Regiment. The majority of these, though, were still in Port Said, with only a few in Wejh, Mecca and Rabegh.

Colonel Brémond, commanding officer of the French Mission. (Bailloud Collection, SHD, Vincennes, via Murphy)

House of the French Military Mission at Wejh. (Bailloud Collection, SHD, Vincennes, via Murphy)

Table 15: Hashemite Armies, 1918

Unit	Allied Forces/Sub-Units	Strength	Notes
Northern Army	Bedouins	6,000	northern Hejaz and Vilayet Syria; led by Prince Faisal; deputy Prince Zaid ibn Husseinn
	Huwaitát		
	Beni Ali		
	Bali		
	Juhainah		
	'Ataiba		
Regulars		2,000	led by al-Masri, then by Pasha al-Askari; Chief-of-Staff Nuri al-Said
1st Division	2 battalions	800	Brigadier-General Amin al-Asil
2nd Division	2 battalions	800	Lieutenant-Colonel Majid Hasun
	2 artillery batteries		8 guns, 150 troops
	Machine gun Detachment		
	1 battalion, Hejaz Camel Corps		
	Mounted Infantry Battalion		mounted on mules
Operation Hedgehog			Colonel P. C. Joyce, then Colonel Alan Dawney
	1 company, Imperial Camel Corps	300	
	Hejaz Company		Rolls-Royce armoured cars
	Hejaz Battery		Talbot cars with 10Pdrs.
Southern Army			Medina area; led by Prince Ali
Bedouins	Arab tribes of centre and southern Hejaz	7,500	
Regulars		1,500	
	2 infantry battalions		
	1 mounted infantry battalion		mounted on mules
	1 camel-mounted infantry battalion		
	4 artillery batteries		
	1 engineering company		
Eastern Army			East of Medina area; led by Prince Abdullah
	Arab tribes	8,000	
Regulars		1,000	
	2 camel-mounted infantry battalions		
	1 cavalry squadron		
	1 mountain artillery battery		
French Military Mission	Mixed Cavalry Marching Regiment	47 officers and 1,127 other ranks	led by Colonel Brémond

Deeply overshadowed by the operations of the Army of the North, Faysal's two other armies, of the South and of the East, did not stand idle for the rest of the First World War. On the contrary, they were involved in several intensive operations.

In March 1917, and again in autumn of the same year, the Ottoman garrison of Medina – reinforced by a tribal contingent of the Rashidis – sortied in a western direction. Indeed, Fakhri Pasha would only be forced to surrender Medina – by his own troops – two months after the Mudros Armistice: on 9 January 1919. He went into captivity together with 456 officers, 9,364 other ranks, and the Albatross serial number AK30. He not only defended Medina well after the end of the First World War, but as he left Medina by train Fakhri took with him several relics of the Prophet (he seemingly abandoned the idea of desecrating Prophet Muhammad's grave) and brought them to Constantinople, where they remain until today. This promptly converted him into a national hero for the Ottomans.

That said, there is no denial that as of 1918, the Hashemite family had achieved all of Sharif Hussein's objectives. Its armies controlled all of the Hejaz and most of the former Vilayet of Syria (including Palestine), and they were soon to be recognised internationally as the rulers of these lands – except for Syria and Palestine. Correspondingly, the First World War ended with ibn Saud not only failing to participate in a more active fashion, but facing a rival family to the north and west. This rival operated a far more powerful army than his own, controlled areas that were far richer than those under his control, and enjoyed British financial and military support. Unsurprisingly, much of the powers abroad now expected all the Arab lands outside of what the British and French claimed as their 'mandates', to soon unify under the Hashemites.[15]

Arab cavalry in the service of the Ottomans forming a Hamidie Regiment equipped with non-traditional heavy lances. Perhaps the Rashidis also formed one of them. (Uyar and Ericksson)

General Fakhri Pasha, commander of the Medina garrison, who surrendered only after the end of the Great War, in January 1919. While evacuating via train, he also took away several relics of the Prophet Muhammed to Constantinople, becoming a national hero. (Martyrs Memorial Museum of Amman, via Dr. David Nicolle)

IBN SAUD DURING THE ARAB REVOLT

Back on 20 November 1916, in the presence of Cox, ibn Saud was knighted in Kuwait, during a military reception organised and run in the style of the Indian Rajas. Also present was Jaber, the new Sheikh of Kuwait (Mubarak passed away a year earlier), as well as Muhammera of Persia, the Sheikh of al-Hasa, and dignitaries from southern Iraq. Arguably, the British forced ibn Saud to accept the supremacy of the Sharif of Mecca, but in turn they also increased their financial aid to GBP 5,000 a month, provided another 3,000 rifles and – what was of particular interest to The Leopard – four machine guns. They may have been of interest, but at that time none of Saud's warriors knew how to operate the machine guns. Nevertheless, he was grateful enough to promise to maintain a force of 4,000 to keep the Rashidis in check, and prevent the arrival of Ottoman reinforcements. Following this, The Leopard was invited by the British to Basra, to see an aircraft flying for the first time, to travel by train and car, and make several x-rays of his own hand – western technological advances, all of which greatly fascinated him.

All this being so, both the Sheikh of Kuwait – furious about a British-imposed blockade of his ports – and ibn Saud were playing a double, if not a triple game. Throughout 1917, Salim not only welcomed the anti-Saud Ajman rebels, but also continued providing supplies to the Ottomans – and this an act actually in collaboration with the Sauds. In September 1917, for instance, a caravan of 3,000 Saudi camels left Qasim for Kuwait, loaded supplies, travelled back to Qasim, and from there marched for Medina – all of this with permission from ibn Saud's eldest son, Turki ibn Abdul Aziz. At the same time, the Sauds took the opportunity to tax the Awazim, who were actually the subjects of the Sheikh of Kuwait. Unable to do much about this 'chaos', the British merely kept an eye on developments. While continuing the naval blockade of Kuwait, they sent a new representative to The Leopard: Brigadier Harry St John Philby.[16]

Harry St John Bridger Philby, famous Arabist and representative of the British Empire to the Saudi court. He became one of the main counsellors of ibn Saud during the next 35 years. His son was later famous also for spying for the Soviets and defecting to Moscow. (Philby, 1948, via Sander)

Young Turki, son of ibn Saud, still as a child, in a picture from 1911 taken by Shakespear. Seven years later he would command a fake blockade of the Ottomans in Kuwait – until his death by the 'Spanish Flu'. (Photo by Shakespear, 1911, via Sander)

BRIGADIER PHILBY

Philby was very intelligent and cultivated, but also eccentric, cynical, and in possession of few social skills. He despised all those who did not share his views, despite the fact that his views usually used to be correct. Philby would remain with ibn Saud for the next 35 years, eventually converting to Islam.[17] His first goal was to effect an alliance between ibn Saud and the Sharif of Mecca, as well as between ibn Saud and Kuwait, and to help The Leopard successfully conclude his war with the Rashidis. Simultaneously, he requested London support ibn Saud with GBP 50,000 for the next six months; send four cannons and their crews, as well as 10,000 rifles. In return, ibn Saud promised to keep 15,000 of his warriors under arms – even if this was probably a significantly overenthusiastic commitment.

Philby at first attempted to open a communication channel to Mecca. Afterwards, he tried to unblock communications between the Hejazis of Mecca and the Saudis of Riyadh, as both leaders refused to send emissaries to each other. The issue was that Sharif Hussein had not given Philby permission to visit him. So, when Philby arrived, he showed to the world that, in reality, the claims made by Hussein that the journey between Mecca and Riyadh was too dangerous were false. Embarrassed, Hussein not only refused to meet him, but also issued no permission for him to enter Mecca. Therefore, Philby did not enter, and was forced to return to ibn Saud by way of a long detour.

By the time he made it back, in April 1918, other British emissaries had 'informed' The Leopard to cancel his assault on the Rashidis. Essentially, the War Office in London was concerned that the weapons and money provided to ibn Saud would be used against

A picture of Philby (foreground, mounted on camel) during his unauthorised 1917 trip to the Hejaz, where he attempted to visit the Sharif of Mecca. It was an enterprise that, from a political point of view, ended in a disaster. (Royal Geographic Society, via Almana)

their ally, the Sharif of Mecca, instead. However, this 'informing' had a diametrically opposite effect on British interests: if they could not attack the Rashidi, then the Ikhwan began pressing ibn Saud to attack the Sharif of Mecca. Upon learning of this development, Philby skipped all other instructions from London and promised to pay GBP 20,000 if ibn Saudi would attack the Rashidis.

Therefore, in August 1918, ibn Saud led his army of some 4,000-6,000 warriors against Häil via Buraida, intending to finish off his archenemies once and forever. While on the way to the city, they captured an enormous amount of booty, giving them confidence for the fight ahead. Häil, however, turned out to be perfectly prepared for defence. The Ikhwan, who made up the majority of Saud's troops, launched several fierce attacks, but were beaten back every time. Eventually, in December 1918, The Leopard gave up and returned to Riyadh.

On the positive side for ibn Saud, he received the promised GBP 20,000. However, the money arrived together with an epidemic – the so-called 'Spanish Flu'. This quickly spread, taking the lives not only of thousands of people living in areas under his control, including much of his army, but also Jauhar, his beloved first wife, and Turki, his eldest son.[18]

The epidemic thus ended the story of ibn Saud's involvement in the Great War – and in entirely unexpected fashion. Between 1914 and 1918, he failed to achieve any of his objectives. Not only did he never manage to defeat the Rashidis, but he failed to openly side with the British against the Ottomans, and then had to watch as both the Hashemites rose to dominance, and his own reign suffered from an epidemic, a factor totally out of his control. Rubbing salt into an injury, in October 1918, Hejazis supported by Sharif Hussein exploited ibn Saud's absence to attack western Nejd, further fomenting animosity – and also making it clear: only one of them would take control of all of the Arabian Peninsula.[19]

5

FIRST SAUDI-HASHEMITE WAR, 1918–1919

While ibn Saud was organizing his army against Häil and negotiating British support, the Hashemites of the Hejaz, under the Sharif Hussein ibn Ali, conducted a punitive operation against an ally of the Sauds. It all began in Khurma, a town of 4,000-5,000 inhabitants on the border between the Hejaz and the Nejd, 170km east of Mecca. Although belonging to a district controlled by the Hashemites since around 1908, the local population had accepted conversion to Wahhabism. The reaction of the Hashemites was to demand that the people return to the orthodox faith. It was also said that, early in 1917, Sharif's own son, Abdullah (whom the British eventually enthroned as the first king of Transjordan), had slapped Emir Khalid ibn Luwai in the face, and put him in jail. In November of that year, ibn Luwai rebelled against the Hejazi. In May 1918, this prompted the Sharif of Mecca to send a force of some 800 Bedouins and 82 regular soldiers, with two old cannons and two machine guns, under the Sharif Hamza to subdue them. Hamza stormed Khurma on 1 June, but was repulsed - losing 14 killed and both of his guns. His demoralised force was subsequently disbanded, but the first shots of the Saudi-Hashemite War – also known as the First Nejd-Hejaz War or the al-Khurma Dispute, had now been fired.

In July 1918, the Sharif of Mecca sent another force of 500 soldiers and 1,200 Bedouins, with four cannons and six machine guns, under Shakir ibn Zaid. The contingent of the western section of the ʿAtaiba that was part of that force and was allied with the Hejazi, under the Amir Shakir, was defeated. This stopped the advance.

Fearing a war between the Hashemites and the Sauds, the British intervened, offering arbitration around the issue of Khurma. Shakir's ʿAtaiba refused to withdraw, however, and continued to roam the area. In August they had an encounter with the Ikhwan in Ain Hannu, 25km east of Khurma, already in Saudi territory, and were repelled.

Part of the ʿAtaiba then defected to the Saudis. On 16 September 1918, the leader of the Khurma, ibn Luwai, led his warriors into an attack on the Hejazi ʿAtaiba and defeated them. Indeed, he repeated this exercise in October as well. Ironically, the majority of the inhabitants of Khurma were ʿAtaiba, making this a civil war. This, however, made the issue even more pressing, because this tribe used to dominate the territories from Mecca to Riyadh. Thus, whoever controlled the tribe, controlled a large area of land too.

BATTLE OF TURABA

By October 1918, only the Bedouin or auxiliary forces ran the Hashemite attacks towards the east. Hussein's best forces were still busy fighting the campaign against the Ottomans in Vilayet Syria. However, the fall of Medina on 9 January 1919, freed the third of Sharif Faisal's armies, and the Hashemites promptly began preparations for an attack on Khurma.

In May 1919, a force under Prince Abdullah (future Emir, later the King of Transjordan) marched in that direction. The force comprised perhaps 500 regular soldiers and 850 Bedouin warriors (not the wildly exaggerated 30,000 men with 5,000 regulars alleged in some sources), but it was supported by 10 guns and 20 machine guns. By this time, Khurma was garrisoned by around 2,000 Ikhwan of the ʿAtaiba, and – probably – some militiamen from the city. On 20 May, they attempted to stop the Hashemite advance, but without success. Indeed, on 21 May, Abdullah was already in Turaba, halfway between Mecca and Khurma. He then fell upon the latter, looting the city – and infuriating ibn Saud. The Leopard reacted promptly, mobilising an army of about 10,000-12,000. His only problem was that this was still hundreds of kilometres away from the battlefield.

Hejazi Bedoiuns, with their typical striped robes, similar to those launched against ibn Luwai in 1918-1919. (Casado, via Serga)

Table 16: Battle of Turaba, 25 May 1919

Emirate	Allied Forces	Strength	Notes
Hejaz/Hashemites			led by Prince Abdullah
	Bedouins	850	
	Regulars	500	1-2 infantry battalions, 10 guns, 20 machine guns
Nejd & Hasa/Saud	Khurma Militia	1,000	led by Amir Khalid ibn Luwai
	Ghatghat Ikhwan	1,100	led by Sultan ibn Bijad ibn Humaid
	Qahtan Ikhwan	900	Led by Hamud ibn Umar

The Prince Abdullah, Emir and later King of Transjordan, who was defeated at Turaba in 1919. (Dr. David Nicolle collection)

Prince Abdullah wearing a British uniform with the Hashemite turban. (Dr. David Nicolle collection)

Led by Sultan ibn Bijad ibn Humaid, the vanguard of about 1,100 camel-mounted Ikhwan from the convent of Ghatghat, reinforced by a detachment of the Qahtan of Hamud ibn Umar, advanced quickly. It crossed 450 kilometres of desert in a matter of seven days, to join the militias of Khurma and additional Ikhwan. With his force numbering perhaps as many as 3,000 now, ibn Luwai and ibn Bijad took Abdullah by surprise: they attacked his camp during the night from 25 to 26 May 1919. By now, the Hashemites were making good use of equipment provided by the British: the camp was surrounded by barbed wire; therefore a frontal assault against this was unthinkable. The Saud's commanders followed their leader's tactics, and split their forces into three groups – almost exactly like The Leopard had done against ibn Rashid in 1906. One of the smaller groups – about 300 warriors in total – approached from the north; the other from the west; while the third guarded their own camp in the east. The Ikhwan opened fire at midnight, promptly convincing the Hashemites they were surrounded and that the enemy was already inside the camp. The rather unsurprising result was chaos, chaos in which Abdullah's warriors began shooting at each other. As the confusion spread, the Sauds quickly unified their force and then launched the actual assault, storming the camp. According to some sources they caught and killed many of the Hejazi soldiers still in their tents. It is certain that Prince Abdullah managed to escape, accompanied by only three regulars and about 150 surviving Bedouin, leaving behind – amongst others – the French Army Captain Muhammad Ould Ali Raho, of the 2nd Spahis Regiment. Considering the First World War was over at this point, and the Ottomans had even withdrawn from Medina, this raises the question whether the French Mission was still supporting the Hashemites in relations to that conflict, or if Raho had actually been personally hired to serve with Hussein's regulars?

While this remains unknown, what is certain is that Saud thus won a resounding victory. Nevertheless, he was cautious too: eager not to lose the British support or subsidies, he then ordered Sultan Bijad to stop, and not to invade Hejaz. The final confrontation with the Sharif of Mecca was thus postponed for a more appropriate moment in time.[1]

Arab Army soldiers in 1919. Notable are their bandoliers, turbans, and, surprisingly, large coats, probably worn as protection against freezing nights in the desert. (Martyr´s Memorial Museum, Ammam, via Dr. David Nicolle)

Arab Army regular soldier in Palestine of 1918-19, still wearing the uniform of the Ottoman Army, but now combined with a Hashemite turban: probably similar to the uniform worn by some at the Battle of Turaba. (Martyr´s Memorial Museum, Ammam, via Nicolle)

6

KUWAIT-NEJD WAR, 1918–1920

In the aftermath of the death of Sheikh Mubarak of Kuwait, the confrontation between the new ruler of Kuwait, Prince Salim – who acceded to the throne in February 1917 – and ibn Saud was only a matter of time. This was so, in particular, as the new Sheikh had begun sheltering the Ajmans. It should be kept in mind that Salim was the same Prince who, the previous year, abandoned support for the Sauds in their fight against the Ajmans after arguing with Mohammed, the brother of ibn Saud. Additionally, Salim was not only a follower of an orthodox Islamic sect (which was, actually, even more puritanical than Wahhabism), but also strenuously refused the ibn Saud's faith, and there was a territorial dispute to solve too. This latter issue was amplified by the fact that, in line with the Anglo-Ottoman Treaty of 1913, the Kuwaitis had the right to collect taxes from the tribes – primarily the Mutair, but also the Awazim and others from al-Hasa (like the Ajman) - 200-250km south and west of the capital. The notion of borders between them and the Sauds had never been discussed. There had been no talk about where they would be drawn. Ibn Saud extracted a partial revenge by informing the British about Salim's secret trade deals with the Ottomans: this became the primary reason for the British naval blockade – a blockade which London then continued well past the Mudros Armistice: indeed, it was still maintained into August 1920, causing major problems to Salim. Despite this subterfuge, and as described above, whenever opportune for his interests, ibn Saud also helped Salim circumnavigate this blockade, most notably through enabling Kuwait to continue supplying the Ottoman garrison of Medina.

Tensions between Salim and ibn Saud thus not only remained high, but even increased. This eventually prompted the Kuwaitis to construct a fort in Dohat Balbul, on the coast of the Persian Gulf, approximately halfway from Kuwait City to Bahrain. This caused a 'race' between them and the Sauds to establish and maintain positions that might define future borders. These actions resulted in the conflict also known as the Kuwait-Nejd War. In February 1920, The Leopard 'permitted' the Mutairs to build an Ikhwan convent near the wells of Qariya'llya. Salim reacted by dispatching a force to Hamdn, about 22 kilometres from Qariya, aiming to block his opponent's farther advance. However, Faisal al-Duwaish, the leader of the Ikhawn Mutair, assaulted the Kuwaiti force with between 2,000 and 4,000 warriors and annihilated them. Salim escaped narrowly

Kuwaiti warriors preparing to defend their capital. (RAF Museum)

and, fearing that poorly protected Kuwait City might become ibn Saud's next target, ordered the construction of major fortifications around it. Working feverishly, over the following two months, the Kuwaitis surrounded the city with an eight-meter tall wall built of bricks, and stretching over 6,000 metres in length.

In addition to this fortification, Salim turned to the British with a request for help. While negotiations were going on, al-Duwaish did not wait: on 9 September, he reached Subaihiya, a mere 20 kilometres south of Kuwait City, and, the next morning, fell on Jahra, just 10 kilometres west of Salim's residence. There, the garrison of about 600 Kuwaitis took refugee inside the Qasr al-Ahmar ('Red Fort'), protected by five metre tall walls. The Ikhwan assaulted three times – always by night – reportedly losing up to 800 killed and 800 wounded (compared to the reported 200 Kuwaiti casualties), but without success. With his force being thus greatly debilitated, al-Duwaish was left without a choice but to return to Subaihiya.

While Kuwaiti claims about Saud's casualties during the battle for Jahra are almost certainly exaggerated – it's more likely that al-Duwaish lost 400-600 killed *and* wounded – and this entire affair systematically downplayed in the related mythology ever since – the fact was that the Ikhwan assault on Kuwait was a very serious business: a de-facto war between the future Kingdom of Kuwait and the Kingdom of Saudi Arabia. Unsurprisingly, the British figured out what was at stake and, keen to win Salim back to their side, launched a military intervention. Not only did the Royal Navy under Major More move its warships closer to the coast, but one of its aircraft also dropped an intimidating message over al-Duwaish's positions in Subaihiya. On 26 October 1920, the Saudis withdrew.[1]

The conflict then ended in a way that emphasised the importance of personal relations – especially mutual animosities – rather than serious political interests. On 27 February 1921, Salim suddenly passed away: within a matter of weeks, the rivalry between Kuwait and ibn Saud became a matter of history, and the two signed a declaration of friendship.

Although the conflict did not yield him the control over additional territory, the war with Kuwait still ended in positive fashion for ibn Saud. By May 1921, he was in firm control over the central and southern Nejd again. Thus the *ulema* in Riyadh declared him the Sultan of the Nejd, positioning him above all the local Emirs and Sheikhs of the region. Indeed, the enthroning of ibn Saud as a king enabled him not only to dominate almost everybody within his reach, but also to directly dispute Sharif Hussein's pre-eminence as the leader of the Arabs. Moreover, through the Uqair Protocol (also 'Uqair Convention'), negotiated by the British High Commissioner to Iraq, Percy Cox, and signed on 2 December 1922, boundaries between Iraq, Kuwait and the Sultanate of Nejd were defined. Whilst it must be said Kuwait lost more than two thirds of its territory, it, in turn, was secured against ibn Saud's expansionism, once and forever.

7

CONQUEST OF ASIR, 1920–1923

Another affair occupying ibn Saud in 1921 was the situation in Asir, a state in the south of Hejaz, extending from Jizan (in modern-day Saudi Arabia) and Abha in the north, to Hodeida (in modern-day Yemen) in the south. In the 18th Century, the Sauds ruled the area, before they were overwhelmed by the Egyptians, in 1818. The Asiris continued to resist, eventually prompting the Egyptians to withdraw, in 1840, when the dynasty of al-Ayedh took over control of the central highlands. Generally, the al-Ayedh allied with Sauds, but they refused to subject themselves to their direct control. Instead, the rulers decided to expand on their own into the Tihama lowlands towards the north, provoking a war with the Ottoman Empire. In 1872, the Ottomans not only defeated, but also captured and executed the leader of the al-Ayedh, and established the Sanjak of Abha, as a territory attached to the Vilayet Yemen.[1]

According to the official Saudi history, the population of Asir were Wahhabis until, in the early 19th Century, a Sufi preacher from Morocco, Ahmed ibn al-Idrisi, appeared to spread a more moderate doctrine. In 1909, just as the local population was, 'returning to Wahhabism, and abandoning the Idrisi doctrine', the Italians convinced Sayyid Muhammad ibn Ali al-Idrisi into provoking another war with the Ottomans. As far as can be assessed with hindsight, this is a mix of truth and mythology.

Actually, al-Idrisi's descendants maintained religious control over Asir for most of the 19th Century, and on 24 December 1908, Sayyid Muhammad ibn Ali al-Idrisi proclaimed himself Imam. This prompted many tribes to recognise him as their spiritual leader. Encouraged, al-Idrisi initiated a new, initially spiritual, then armed insurgency against the Ottomans. Through 1909, his warriors took over az-Zaydiyah and al-Luhayyah, forcing the Ottomans into the Treaty of al-Hafa'ir, granting him the position of *Kaymakam* of Asir: a de-facto independent ruler under Ottoman Suzerainty.

In October 1910, the insurgency was renewed amid a dispute over the application of Sharia Law, and Idrisi rebellion spread. The following year, it began receiving Italian support – foremost in the form of arms and ammunition, but also through the naval bombardment of Ottoman-controlled ports, before a Hashemite force under Sharif Hussein – at the time still loyal to the Ottomans – marched into northern Asir and defeated the Idrisid forces.

The fortunes of Asir reversed in 1915 when Muhammad ibn Ali al-Idrisi established contacts with the British administration in Aden. With support from Great Britain, he liberated most of Asir and on 3 August 1917 proclaimed himself the Emir of an independent Idrisid Emirate of Asir, with capitol in Abha. Always keeping an eye on the Imamate of Yemen, the British quickly recognised the sovereignty of Asir. However, because of growing tensions both with Hashemites in the north, and Yemen in the south, al-Idrisi then entered an alliance with ibn Saud. Mere months later, in 1920, he passed away, leaving behind his son, Sayyid Ali ibn Muhammad al-Idrisi al-Hasani, and his brother, Sayyid al-Hasan ibn Ali al-Idrisi al-Hasani in a feud over succession. Eventually, the title of Emir was passed to the former, but he was still a youngster lacking authority. His primary opponent became Hassan al-Ayedh or al Aidh, the leader of tribes in the mountainous area in the centre of Asir, and Emir of Abha: he was not only allied with the Hashemites, but also at odds with the Wahhabis. 'Logically', Prince Sayyid requested ibn Saud's support.

The Saudi governor of Abha going to the Mosque, escorted by his warriors. Abha was the capital of the pro Hejazi Emir al-Ayedh or al Aidh, and enemy of the Wahhabis. It was conquered in 1921-1922 by ibn Saud. (Popperfoto, via Almana)

Officially, explaining he was only interested in mediating between Idrists and al-Ayedh, The Leopard dispatched a force of 3,000 Ikhwan, commanded by his cousin ibn Jiluwi (the former governor of al-Hasa and the assassinator of the governor of Riyadh in 1902), to Asir. Alternative reports cite Abdul Aziz ibn Musaid as commander.

The Ikhwan went into a camp near Bishah, while waiting for al-Ayedh to respond to Musaid's demand to surrender. When Hassan al-Ayedh reacted by sending a package of bullets as the sole answer, Saud's commander launched an attack on the fortified camp in Wadi Hajlah. Commanded by Muhammad bin Abdul Rahman al-Ayedh, the Asiri army proved no match for the Ikhwan and was thoroughly routed. Indeed, the defeat and the capture of Hassan al-Ayedh caused such a panic that the Asiris abandoned even Abha: ibn Musaid was able to conquer the capitol of Asir against very little resistance. The campaign ended there, though, and henceforth Asir was split into two: the Sheikhdom of Upper Asir, with its capital in Abha, and the Emirate of Asir, with capitol in Sabya, and including the port of Hodeida.

After keeping Hassan al-Ayedh in prison for about a year, ibn Saud pardoned the defeated Asiri leader. However, in 1922, the latter entered an alliance with Sharif Hussein and their united armies recaptured Abha. In July 1922, ibn Saud launched another campaign, this time appointing his second son, Prince Faisal – then still a teenager – to lead an army of 6,000 warriors. As they advance in a southwest direction, the corps was reinforced by about 4,000 Bedouins from the Qahtan, Zahran, and Shabran tribes. Together, they defeated the Asiris and Hejazis, secured the oasis of Bisha, and, in September-October 1922, took Abha. Sharif Hussein launched a counterattack in April 1923, but it failed, and a month later Faisal returned to Riyadh with al-Ayedh as his prisoner.

An extremely rare photo of the Imam Yahiya of Yemen, who would dispute Asir with ibn Saud in 1924-1934. (Nicolle´s Collection)

Meanwhile, Emir Idrisi died, leaving his sons to fight between themselves for power in the Emirate of Asir. Imam Yahiya (also 'Yahya of Yemen') intervened and placed one of them, Prince Ali, in power. In 1924, Ali was deposed by his uncle, another Hussein; while Yemen took advantage of the resulting chaos to secure the port of Hodeida, followed by Jizan, another port further north. Because Jizan was his possession, Emir Idrisi requested ibn Saud for help. Through a treaty signed in October 1926, The Leopard secured Asir as an inheritance. Sure enough, he had to wait for eight additional years to defeat Imam Yahya in yet another war (the story of which will be told in Volume 2), but, ultimately, he was able to annex the entire Asir, in 1934.[2]

8

THE END OF THE RASHIDI EMIRATE, 1920–1921

Another affair ibn Saud was able to successfully conclude in the aftermath of the Great War was the fate of the Emirate of Jebel Shammar (also known as the Emirate of Häil, or the Rashidi Emirate). When the Ottoman Empire was dissolved by the British and the French – resulting in the Turkish War of Independence and then the proclamation of the Turkish Republic led by Mustafa Kemal 'Atatürk' – the Rashidi confederation lost material support from Constantinople. By this time, the state was gradually sliding into decline, one that had already begun with the loss of Riyadh, in 1902, and the death of Abd al-Aziz in the battle of Rawdat Muhanna, against ibn Saud, in 1906.

The next Emir, Mutaib (II) ibn Abdulaziz reigned for only a year before he was killed by Sultan bin Hammud, a grandson of Ubayad (and brother of the first Emir). Unsuccessful in fighting the Sauds, he was killed by his own brothers and succeeded by Saud ibn Abdulaziz Hamoud, in 1908. Aged only 10 at the time he was made Emir, Saud ibn Abdulaziz reigned through a relatively peaceful period, but continued losing power. The Wahhabi missionaries were successful in spreading their preaching from Qasim to the Shammar territory, attracting an ever-larger body of followers. Eventually, this left the Rashidi capital of Häil isolated.

The spark that led to the downfall of the Rashidi Emirate was provided by what might first appear as an accident. In 1920, the Emir went hunting and picnicking with his family. When he began laughing at the poor marksmanship of his cousin, Abdullah ibn Talal, the man turned around and killed him on the spot. A few weeks later, 13-years-old Abdullah (II) ibn Mutib was made Emir, to whom the regency council appointed his uncle, Mohammed ibn Talal – a grandson of Naif and the sole surviving son of Talal, the 2nd Rashidi Emir – as the commander of the Shammar Army.

Ibn Talal's first task was to march north and put down the revolt of the Ruwala tribe. This lived in the southern Syrian desert, and since 1914 had taken Jaul and Sakaka. After crossing the Nefud desert, ibn Talal's army recovered both towns. Encouraged by this triumph, he returned to Häil and, in early 1921, deposed and jailed – but not killed, quite surprising given the customs of that time – Abdullah.

When Muhammad (II) ibn Talal climbed to power, it appeared that the Rashidis had finally found a competent, charismatic, and also a humane leader. But, when informed about the disorder and rebellions in the Emirate, ibn Saud did not to give him any respite. In April 1921, he sent Prince Faisal to lead a corps reinforced by al-Duwaish-led Ikhwan of the Mutair tribe. Simultanesouly, he then sent his brother Mohammed to command another force against the Rashidis. Fighting in their usual, merciless fashion, the Ikhwan managed to reach the walls of Häil before ibn Talal caused them heavy losses and forced them to stop their assault. The Leopard then sent another contingent of Bedouin, this time commanded by

The 11th Emir of Shammar, Saud ibn Abdulaziz ibn Rashid, between 1910 to 1920. He was killed by a cousin in a discussion during a picnic. (Unknown photographer)

Prince Saud: this force circumnavigated Häil and secured the oasis of Beqaa, northeast of the capitol. Through May, additional Saud forces continued pouring into the Rashidi Emirate from almost all the corners of the Nejd. Among them was a section of 'Ataiba Ikhwan under ibn Rabian, followed by the bulk of the tribe led by ibn Bijad. As the war went on, on 17 July, the deposed Emir Abdullah ibn Mutib suddenly appeared to announce that he had escaped ibn Talal's prison and requested help from the Sauds. Bewildered, Faisal and Mohammed returned to Riyadh to discuss the situation with ibn

Above: The 12th Emir Abdullah ibn Mitub (or bin Mutaib), barely a 13-year-old child, who was deposed by his uncle ibn Talal, and asked for help from the Sauds. (Unknown photographer)

Right: The last Emir of the Rashidi, Mohammed ibn Talal, a capable and more humane leader, who defeated ibn Saud´s sons but was not able to overcome the arrival of the King Saud with all his army in 1922. (Unknown photographer)

Saud and seek his instructions - leaving only the al-Duwaish's Ikwan group to continue operations against the Rashidi army. Indeed, Duwaish eventually managed to catch up with the elusive Rashidi army in the Juhamiya area, north of Häil. Cornered, Muhammad ibn Talal first pretended to agree to convert to Wahhabism, but during the related ceremony, he and his aides unleashed a surprise attack that shattered Duwaish's court. Although badly bruised, Saud's commander managed to escape the assassination and re-group the bulk of his force before awaiting reinforcements.

Ibn Saud took his time to organise a new campaign. In late August 1921, he set out from Buraida with his brother Mohmammed, Faisal and several other sons, leading an army of up to 10,000, including the Ikhwan of Mutair, 'Ataiba, and Qahtan. The seriousness of this operation can be gauged by the fact that the Sauds even brought with them guns captured from the Ottomans in 1904. Ironically, these were brought into position but did not fire a single shot: it remains unclear if there was anybody around who knew how to operate them, or if they were in much too poor condition for use.

The Sauds reached the area immediately east of Häil on 4 September, and found themselves facing ibn Talal's army. The result was a short but bitter battle in which the Rashidis were defeated, and Talal had to flee the battlefield and find refugee behind the walls of his capital. Ibn Saud ordered al-Duwaish's right hand, Sheikh Mutluq of the Mutair, to assault the city walls with his force. The Ikhwan moved out and charged. Mutluq thus had the horror of seeing his men shot down while courageously rushing to the wall, or killed while thrown from assault ladders, whilst never losing the belief in promises of the *Ulema* - that they would enter Paradise if killed in combat. However, after the first and then the second of his assaults both failed with heavy losses, Mutluq began developing doubts. Indeed, he went as far as to challenge the *Ulema*: if such a prize was meant for everyone, he argued, why were the members of *Ulema* not the first to the walls? Eventually, none other than ibn Saud was forced to rebuke him for destroying the faith of the Ikhwan.

With both assault attempts failing, The Leopard decided to attack in a different fashion. His aides were in contact with the as-Saban family – followers of the deposed Emir who resided within the city limits. During the evening, they opened the gates of the city, in exchange for a guarantee the civilian population would be spared and there would be no looting. This let ibn Saud and 2,000 of his warriors, to enter Häil. Taken by surprise and overwhelmed, ibn Talal remained defiant: together with his closest aides, he retreated

Above: Prince Faisal (later on, the third King of Saudi Arabia), a capable leader that led the Saudi forces in the conquest of Asir, then against the Rashidi in 1922 (failing), after that the rebel 'Ataiba Ikhwans, and finally defeating Yemen in the 1934 War. He was killed by a member of the Araif family in 1975. (Kheirallah, 1952, via Sander).

Right: Ibn Saud on horse in 1922, during the Oqair Conference. He would have had a similar appearance when arriving with the main army for the conquest of Häil in 1921. (Dickson, 1922, via Sander)

into the citadel. There followed lengthy negotiations, and it was only on 4 November 1921 that ibn Talal agreed to surrender on condition of his life being spared so he could reunite with family members exiled in Riyadh.

To demonstrate his power but also his ties with the Rashidi and at least attempt to justify his rights over the Emirate of Shammar, ibn Saud married ibn Talal's wife, Nur bint as-Saban – a member of the family that had opened the doors of Häil to him. In turn, one of ibn Talal's daughters married Prince Mua'id ibn Abdulaziz al-Saud's 15th son: they were latter to become parents of Prince Faisal ibn Musa'id, the assassin of King Faisal. The new governor of what was now another province of the Sultanate of Nejd was ibn Julwi, Saud's cousin who had just returned from his own triumph in Asir.[1]

Thus, after 19 years of struggle, the Saud finally defeated and integrated its archenemies, the Rashidi, and was the master and lord of all the Nejd. This would represent one of the swords of Saud: the Kingdom of Nejd.

Of course, it was still a far cry from unifying all of Arabia. Indeed, while The Leopard was busy with Kuwait, Asir, and the Rashidis, the Hashemites remained at large in the Hejaz. Indeed, sons of Sharif Hussein were enthroned as the kings of Transjordan and Iraq – two entirely new nations, both carved out of former Ottoman provinces by the pens of British and French officials. Thus, the final struggle for Arabia was to become one between the Sauds and the Hashemites. For ibn Suad, this required defeating an army massively bolstered by the British during the Great War, and the conquest of the Hejaz – the second sword of ibn Saud – with the two holiest places of Islam: Mecca and Medina. Considering that as of 1921-1924, the Sultanate of Nejd was, unlike its enemies, not supported by any major foreign power, the chances of victory for such an enterprise certainly appeared slim. Just how The Leopard achieved this feat is to be told in the Volume 2.[2]

BIBLIOGRAPHY

BOOKS
Al-Rasheed, Madawi, *Politics in an Arabia Oasis* (I.B. Tauris, 1997)
Almana, Mohammed, *Arabia Unified* (Hutchinson Benham, 1982)
Bearman, P., Bianquis, T., Bosworth C.E., van Donzel, E., and Heinrichs, W.P., *The Encyclopaedia of Islam* (Leiden: Brill, 2007)
Bowyer, Chazz, *RAF Operations 1918-1938* (London: William Kimber & Co., 1988)
Cooper, Tom & Sipos, Milos, *Wings of Iraq, Volume 1* (Warwick: Helion & Co., 2020)
De Gaulle, Charles, *La France et son Armée* (Tempus Perrin, 2016)
Eriksson, Edward J., *Defeat in Detail* (Praeger, 2003)
Glubb, John Baggot, *War in the Desert* (London: Hodder & Stoughton, 1960)
Halley, J., *The Squadrons of the RAF* (Tonbridge, Kent: Air Britain (Historians) Ltd, 1980)
Mickaberidze, Alexander, *Conflict and Conquest in the Islamic World: A Historical Encyclopedia, 2 Vols* (ABC-Clio, 2011)
Murphy, Dr David, *The Arab Revolt* (Oxford: Osprey Publishing 2008)
Nicolle, Dr David; and Air Vice Marshall Ali Gbar, Gbar, *Air Power and the Arab World, Vol 1, 3 and 4* (Helion & Company, 2019)
Provence, Michael, *The Last Ottoman Generation and the Making of the Modern Middle East*, (San Diego: Cambridge University Press, 2017)
Sabini, John, *Armies in the Sand: The Struggle for Mecca and Medina* (London: Thames and Hudson Ltd., 1981)
Sander, Nestor, *ibn Saud: King by Conquest* (Selwa Press, 2008)
Vassiliev, Alexei, *The History of Saudi Arabia* (New York: NYU Press, 2000)
Uyar, Mesut & Eriksson, Edward J., *A Military History of the Ottomans: From Osman to Attaturk.* (Santa Barbara, California: ABC CLIO, LLC, 2009)

JOURNAL ARTICLES
Alexander, Group Captain John, 'Hot Air, Aeroplanes and Arabs: T. E. Lawrence and Air Power', *Air Power Review* magazine, Vol. 22, No. 1, spring 2019 (Royal Air Force)
Casado, Alfonso, ´La Legión Árabe Combate en Jordania´. *Serga* magazine No. 85 (In Spanish)
Leclerc, Christophe, `La guerrilla durante la Revuelta Árabe´ *Desperta Ferro Contemporánea,* magazine, No. 20 (Madrid: Desperta Ferro, 2017) (In Spanish)

OTHER PRINT RESOURCES
Royal Air Force Museum, *The Royal Air Force and Kuwait* (PDF handout)

WEBSITES
Allday, Louis, 'A Drunken Russian Pilot and the Bombing of Mecca, 1925', blogs.bl.uk, accessed 9 September 2016
D'Andurain, 2017. 'Enffondrement Du Rêve d 'un Royaume Arabic Independent', orientxxi.info
Hassard, David & Downey, Bill, 'The Week by Week Story of the Sopwith Aviation Compöany and its Products through 1916', *KingstonAviation.org*
Henderson, Captain Thomas, 'The exploits of "C" Flight 14Th Squadron R.F.C.', rogersstudy.co.uk
Sherzad, Tim, 'How Russians Bombed Mecca', *en.topwar.ru*, accessed 5 February 2019

NOTES

Chapter 1
1. Sander, pp.11-18. Nura was ibn Saud´s favourite sister. Glubb, p.55. Almana, pp.35-37. Vassiliev, p.212. The nickname 'The Leopard' appears in the title of a novel by the Spanish writer Alberto Vázquez Figueroa.
2. Glubb, pp.25-34
3. Glubb, pp.25-34
4. Glubb, pp.25-34.
5. Glubb, pp.25-34. Murphy, pp.21, 23, 25. Vassiliev, p.211. These figures for soldiers and their bibliographical sources will be given throughout this work, but they are based mainly on Glubb and Vassiliev, and to a lesser extent, on Sander and Murphy.
6. Sander, pp.201-212, and 4-9. The date of birth of ibn Saud remains controversial: it was thought to be in 1880, but ibn Saud laughed about this saying that he had been robbed of four years of life. The correct date seems to be 1876, but other sources say 1875 or 1877, too. Regarding the number of Saudi-Kuwaiti warriors in 1901, most of sources cite these as 10,000. With the Sauds in exile their resources and allies were scarce, and the Kuwaitis did not have enough potential to equip such a large army. The sources cite five tribal contingents, which could number 1,000 warriors each – at most. It should be kept in mind that in 1930, ibn Saud gathered 16 tribal or city contingents, and the number of fighters was 16,000. Glubb, pp.41-54. Vassiliev, pp.210-212.

Chapter 2
1. Sander, pp.18-20. Almana, p.41-44, for the anecdote of the scorpion and Kuwait´s changed letters. Vassiliev, pp.214-215, turns the battle of Dilam into a series of skirmishes in September and October 1902.
2. Sander, pp.20-21, is the one who gives us more details of the operations. Almana, pp.44-45. Vassiliev, pp.215-216.
3. While the exact status of Ottoman Army units in Mesopotamia as of 1904 remains unclear, primarily because the entire service underwent a major reform following the Young Turk Revolution and the establishment of the Second Constitutional Era, in June 1908, it should be kept in mind that even as of 1914, the Ottoman Army structure in the Vilayets Baghdad and Mosul was still underdeveloped. Despite establishment of the usual – empire-wide – network of major military educational facilities, and regular recruiting of Arab, Christian, even Jewish and other ethnic groups (see Provence, *The Last Ottoman Generation*, for details), the build-up of home-based units in Mesopotamia lagged behind. Nominally established in 1877, and responsible for all of Mesopotamia, as of 1904-1908, the Ottoman VI Army included the 6th, 11th, and 12th Infantry Divisions, and the 15th Artillery Brigade, as well as four reserve divisions. However, by 1914, the situation was reversed and many assets withdrawn, leaving an entirely different composition. Mosul served as the headquarters of the XII Corps (35th and 36th

Divisions), and Baghdad headquartered the XIII Corps (37th and 38th Divisions). In turn, their major sub-units were understrength (indeed, the 38th Division was existent in cadre form only). Once the Ottoman Empire entered the First World War, the majority of these units were re-deployed to other fronts, leaving behind only the 35th Division. The 38th Division was worked-up by the summer of 1915 (but then re-deployed elsewhere) together with the newly established 45th Division. This is why, and although all the cavalry units of the Ottoman Army were officially disbanded in 1908, in 1914-1915 a 'Provisional Division' came into being, including the 1st and 2nd Tribal Cavalry Brigades. These units were primarily responsible for the defence of the area south of Baghdad. See also the next note.

4   Sander, pp.21-26. For the Harab, 2,000 warriors were those provided to ibn Saud when they were under his rule as part of the Ikhwan. Concerning the Ottomans, Sander (pp.21-26) lists six battalions and 2,400 troops. Ar-Rasheed (*Politics in an Arabia oasis*, p.124), mentions four regiments of 600 soldiers each. Almana (p.45), mentions eight Ottoman Army battalions. Vassiliev (pp.217-218), speaks of eight or even eleven battalions and 2,400 troops. It seems that there is no information based on contemporary Ottoman sources: even the excellent and in-depth work by Mesut and Eriksson only fleetingly mentions these campaigns and units in Yemen, as well as the protection of the railway to Mecca – but no combat against ibn Saud. Erickson (Defeat in the Detail, p.17), mentioned the VI Army as headquartered in Baghdad and composed of two quadrangular divisions (four regiments each) – the 11th and 12th – but also the 6th Cavalry Division and the 15th Artillery Brigade, as of 1908. Assuming that these units were there four years earlier, the Ottoman Army might have sent the 11th and/or 12th Divisions. Regarding casualties, Vassiliev quoted these based on Rashidi chronicles. In turn, Saudi sources usually mention 5,000 warriors on their side, which coincides with '1,000 each' for every tribal contingent. It is more likely that about 3,000 were led by ibn Saud, while 1,000-2,000 came from Buraida and Mutair. The number of 2,000 Rashidi horsemen is based on the fact that ibn Saud dared to attack them, and was also able to repel his enemy's attack – which is likely indicative of his numerical superiority. On the contrary, the usual Saudi figure for 15,000 Rashidis and Ottomans is unrealistic.

5   Sander, pp.21-26. Regarding Shunana, the figures of 10,000 Sauds versus 25,000 Rashidies are unrealistic. With such a numerical difference, Saudi victory would have been impossible. The figure of 190 Ottoman troops killed by the Rashidi allies in Shunana is also not deserving of confidence, because it was impossible for anyone to bother in the middle of a battle with counting the dead, and then – amid a de-facto defeat – separating these from those killed in fighting with the Sauds immediately after. As for the story of the Rashidis attacking their Ottoman allies, at first it seems unbelievable, but it was described by two Ottoman survivors of the battle to a British agent in the Gulf, and the stories circulating in Constantinople were similar. Therefore, it at least deserves the benefit of the doubt. Glubb (pp.56-57), reduced the Ottoman force to 2,000 men, and only mentioned the battle of Bukairiya, adding 1,000 dead per each side. He did not mention the second battle, though: only that the Ottoman force was reduced to about 700. It is possible that he confused two battles into just one, which in turn means that his numbers of Ottoman casualties – and survivors – refer to the combination of two clashes. Vassiliev (pp.217-218), placed the assault on ibn Rashid's convoy in al-Bukairiya. He only mentioned several dozen casualties, probably referring to the attack on the convoy alone while omitting all the subsequent actions.

6   Sander (pp.26-30), and Glubb (pp.56-57), speak about Ottoman troops dispatched in January 1905, so the April figure at Buraida probably includes all these January reinforcements, as well as the survivors of the 1904 campaign (about 700). The figures of 3,000, 750 and 700, match the 4,500 present in Buraida. Additional details are based on Vassiliev (pp.219-220). It remains unknown what Ottoman Army units were sent to Qasim. Mesut, in conversation with the author, stated, 'there was one field army (the VII) in Yemen and an independent division (the 16th Hejaz Division) in the Hejaz region. Before 1911 the Ottoman army was using square unit formation, which means every division had two brigades and every brigade had two regiments. So the 16th Hejaz Division's brigades were the 31st Brigade (61st and 62nd regiments) and the 32nd Brigade (63rd and 64th regiments). That division had a Jager battalion and a field artillery regiment (with two battalions). It also had 9 fortress artillery batteries. The Hejaz Railway was protected by two railway battalions and a railway engineering and repair battalion. The VII Army comprised the 13th (25th and 26th brigades) and the 14th Divisions (27th and 28th brigades), the 7th Cavalry Regiment and the 7th Artillery Regiment. It also had some fortress artillery'. As some of the Ottoman troops were sent from Medina (by the Hejaz railway), they probably included elements of the 16th Division. Certainly enough, Erickson appears to contradict this by stating (in Defeat in Detail, p.17), that in 1908, the VII Army (13th and 14th Divisions, and the Cavalry Brigade) was in Arabia, while the 16th Division was in Yemen.

7   Sander, pp.26-30. Although they agree on essential details, there are several versions about the death of ibn Rashid. Howarth does not mention the banner: only that ibn Rashid was killed while trying to cheer his own men during a stormy dawn. Philby claims that ibn Rashid was in another camp adding reinforcements and when he as he prepared to launch a counterattack, he mistakenly entered a Saudi camp and was killed. This coincides with Rihani. Ibn Saud's force was small, so it is probably true that the Rashidis were divided into several camps, otherwise The Leopard's decision to attack them would have been suicidal. On the other hand, several Arab sources agree on the story of the banner taken by the Sauds and this confusion led to ibn Rashid's death. That said, Almana (pp.46-49) quotes an eyewitness who recalled that ibn Saud's standard bearer dropped the flag: this is why the author has followed that version. The same source also described the previous strategy of avoiding direct clashes and seeking to annul the wells of the other. Finally, Almana claims that the Rashidis had 20,000 men, with 2,500 horsemen among them. This appears massively exaggerated: as will be described in Volume 2, even as of 1930, the ex-Rashidis – when serving with ibn Saud's forces – were providing a mere 4,000 warriors. Considering other sources state that ibn Rashid had a lower number of warriors on hand than usual, it is more likely that he only commanded about 2,500 cavalry, as quoted by Almana. Glubb (pp.56-57) mentions the attack in the middle of a sandstorm. Vassiliev (pp.219-220) quotes the Rashidi chronicles, according to which ibn Rashid tried to restore order in the middle of the combat and moved to his banner – until discovering, to his horror – that he had run straight into the Saud's centre that had taken his banner. To this author, that appears as the most likely explanation.

8   Sander, pp.30-32 and Glubb, p.57, for the Ottoman subsidies. Additional details by Almana, pp.53-55. Vassiliev (pp.222-224) seems to infer that Buraida never surrendered to Saud – at least not before May 1908 - while Sander seems to have concluded that the city surrendered and then revolted again, and that several times. The Ottoman units, according to Mesut´s feedback, were probably elements of the 16th Division (based in the Hejaz).

9   Sander, pp.30-32. Glubb, p.57. Almana, pp.53-55. Almana is the only one who quotes, briefly, the battle of Asha'alan. Vassiliev, pp.222-224, for the composition of the Rashidi and Saudi forces. The sequence of events of al-Duwaish's second rebellion is not very clearly explained: Vassiliev seems to involve him in the second battle of Trufiyah, while Sander seems to indicate that he fought it a little earlier, so there were two battles of Truffiyah.

10 Vassiliev, pp.222-224. Ottoman forces as reported by Mesut.

Chapter 3

1. Sander, pp.32-34, is the only source providing details of this period of internal rebellions. Vassiliev, p. 224-7, is the only source to point out the double game of Mubarak and the Zafirs, as well as the clashes with the Hejazis.
2. Sander, pp.34-36. Glubb, p.58. Almana, p.55. Vassiliev (pp.227-231), gives a more detailed explanation of the organization of the Ikhwan, its founders, the catalogue of convents, their separation between warriors and non-warriors, etc. He also dates their establishment with early 1913. The estimate of one flag per convent and a hundred warriors per flag comes from this author: it is based on the work for the Volume 2, including several estimates for the number of Ikhwan in their attacks on Iraq, but especially their rebellion against ibn Saud, in 1929-1930.
3. Sander, pp.37-39, 112-115, 250-251, 188-189 is the only source to provide a detailed narration on the operations and negotiations. Many authors – including those working for the government of the Kingdom of Saudi Arabia – reject the signing of this Ottoman-Saudi Treaty within the context of a border dispute with Oman. Almana, pp.55-56 and Vassiliev, pp.231-232, for the Ottoman threats and the revenues of al-Hasa. Information about the Ottoman planned counterattack for 1914, has been provided by Mesut.

Chapter 4

1. Sander, pp.41-43, 251-52. The known figures for the number of Bedouin warriors offer a point of orientation for an estimate on the size of each contingent: about 800. Glubb (p.58-59), mentions the Shammari infantry pushing the Saudi infantry, while the cavalry wings of the latter were defeating the Rashidis. Almana (pp.56-57), Vassiliev (p.237) and Sander agree with the number of militia citizens of the Nejd (about 1,500). Vassiliev claims that those of the Rashidis were also about 1,500, but he probably refers only to the citizens of Häil, and not to the entire army. He also speaks of 100 casualties per side. The rest of the Rashidi troops would be similar in number, although somewhat inferior to the Saudis, perhaps 4,000 men in all, as had been usual for the Emirate of Häil when it was in the hands of Saud, for example in 1930. For some Arab sources, however, it would be only 1,500 or 1,800 Rashidi warriors, against about 2,000 Saudis.
2. Sander, pp.43-45. Vassiliev, p.253 for the Saudi policy to disperse the Ajman. Also, as we will see, the rebel Ajman were around 2,000 in 1929-1930.
3. Murphy, pp.7-8, 21, 27, 32-33.
4. Murphy, pp.20-21. The Saudi pay for levies was at the rate of GBP 3 in gold for each soldier per month, and 6 for the chiefs and officers. We have estimated that the same or similar amounts would be paid for the Hejazis. On the other hand, ibn Saud promised the British a total of 15,000 warriors in exchange for 50,000 GBP. That is, at the rate of GBP 3.3 per warrior per month, this must include the payments of the chiefs and officers, which being double that of the soldiers indicates that the first were around 5% of the total troops. Thus, GBP 30,000 from the beginning of the war would, at most, result in the recruitment of 9,000 warriors. On the other hand, the GBP 220,000 monthly paid by the British to the Hashemites was enough for not more than the famous 30,000 men of the regular Arab Army – although it should have been enough for 66,000 of them. So, it seems that almost half of this money went to pay for ammunition, weapons, equipment, and food, not to mention that some of it ended up in pockets of the Hashemite family. When, in 1925, Sharif Husayn fled the Hedjaz, he carried with him a fortune of GBP 800,000 - in gold. On the other hand, the number of tribes cited in the service of the Hejazis at the beginning of the war is ten, which brings us back to about 10,000 Bedouins in total, at most. This figure coincides with the number of Hashemite rifles at the end of 1916, according to Vassiliev (p.244).
5. For details, see Provence, *The last Ottoman Generation*. Murphy, pp.20-21.
6. Murphy, p.27, pp.34-35. *Desperta Ferro*, map, p.8 and 22. Leclerc, pp.20-21. The Ottoman battalions and cavalry regiments isolated in the last corner of the Empire and surrounded by deserts, would have had a very small number of troops each, between 400 and 800 men at most. That is why Fakhri's options *vis-à-vis* the Arabs were slimmer than they seemed. For the aviation, see Alexander, 'Hot Air, Aeroplanes and Arabs' & Hassard et all, 'The Week by Week Story of the Sopwith Aviation Company…'.
7. Murphy, p.35-36, 27.
8. Nicolle, Vol 1 (Vol 21), pp.77-79. For British aviation, see Henderson and Alexander, 'Hot Air, Aeroplanes and Arabs'.
9. The information about the Royal Navy's seaplanes embarked aboard HMS *Ben-my-Chree* and HMS *Raven II* is based on the excellent article 'The Week by Week Story of the Sopwith Aviation Company and its Products through 1916', posted on the website KingstonAviation.org. Sadly, the exact complement of each of two Royal Navy's seaplane tenders remains unclear. What is known that the slightly larger HMS *Ben-My-Chree* usually embarked two Schneiders and up to four of larger, but folding-wing Short floatplanes. The smaller HMS *Raven II* could carry only four.
10. Alexander, 'Hot Air, Aeroplanes and Arabs'.
11. Ibid. Murphy, pp.36-39. Desperta Ferro, map p.22. Nicolle, pp.79-80 for the Ottoman aviation.
12. Murphy, pp.36-39. Desperta Ferro, map p.22. Nicolle, pp.79-80 for the Ottoman aviation. The aerial actions were not narrated in relation to the ground operations, so the author of this work has tried to tell them interwoven with such ground actions. For the British aviation, see Henderson and Alexander.
13. Murphy, pp.46-49, 53-54. Nicolle, p.81 for the Ottoman aviation. Nicolle cites a Pfalz P8 among those retired, but more likely this is a mistake and refers to the P10, whose operations were narrated several times. For the British Aviation, see Henderson and Alexander.
14. Rather ironically, the duo al-Askari and as-Saad went on to serve Faisal during the short-lived Arab Kingdom of Syria. Following the French invasion of the latter, they were forced to flee to Iraq, where in early 1921, al-Askari was appointed the Minister of Defence, while as-Saad served as the Chief-of-Staff of the newly-established Army (and, years later, as the Prime Minister in several governments). Despite their good reputation as commanders, precisely because of their loyalty to the British, they experienced immense problems in building-up the Iraqi Army, primarily because although there were thousands of highly-experienced veterans of the Ottoman Army available, next to nobody wanted to serve in a, de-facto, British controlled military service, nor to undergo the related British (re)training and indoctrination courses. On the contrary, as repeatedly stressed by Provence (in *The Last Ottoman Generation*), and contrary to countless other reports ever since, not one Arab officer defected from the Ottoman Army during the First World War. The few officers that served with Sharif Faisal's Arab Army, and then with the Arab Kingdom of Syria Army had been captured during the Palestine Campaign of 1917-1918, and then convinced to join Faysal while interned in prisoner of war camps. The mass of others joined Faisal only after the Mudros Armistice (which ended the Ottoman involvement in the First World War).
15. Murphy, pp.26, 38, 68 and 73. Nicolle, pp.81-84 for the Ottoman aviation. The data regarding the Albatross and the Rumpler that remained in Medina are somewhat confusing, since both aircraft are cited in Ma'an, in the month of July, although then they are also cited again in Medina, later on, and then - the Rumpler – in Ma'an again, since 18 January.
16. Sander, pp.45-47. Vassiliev, p.245.
17. Notably, Brigadier Philby was also the father of famous Kim Philby, one of 'Cambridge Five', who would end up spying for the Union of Soviet Socialist Republics (USSR; colloquially 'Soviet Union') during the Cold War.
18. Originating from Kansas, in the United States of America, the

epidemic spread wherever there were large concentrations of humans: initially on passenger ships carrying troops of the US Army to France, then in the trenches and overcrowded hospitals of the Great War, and then into the cities all over Europe and the USA. By 1921, nearly a third of the global population – an estimated 500 million people – had been infected. Ironically, no country has ever officially recognised this epidemic as such, let alone given it a name. Indeed, the information about its spread was severely curtailed by censors in the belligerent countries (to maintain morale), regardless of how overwhelmed authorities were. Solely the Spanish government – which remained neutral throughout the First World War – and the local newspapers, not only detected the epidemic but warned the population, and began reporting about its outbreak. This is why it became known as the 'Spanish Flu'.

19 Sander, pp.48-49, 253-258. Almana, pp.57-58, 80-84 and 90. Almana provides details of the King's clothes being cut. Vassiliev, p.246 and 248. The Saudi army has been estimated based on the price paid by Philby, which is the same price for which Saud offered 4,000 men, or at the rate of GBP 3.3 a month per soldier and officer (for about 6,000 men at most). In fact, Mickaberidze (p.800) speaks of 5,000 warriors.

Chapter 5

1 Sander, pp.49-50, gives a very detailed account of the operations, and speaks of 800 warriors under ibn Zaid. Vassiliev, pp.248-249, speaks of 500 regulars and 1,200 Bedouins in ibn Zaid's expedition. Sander cites 4,000 Ikhwan of the ′Ataiba – which appears rather over enthusiastic – and another 1,100 as reinforcements. However, Almana speaks of only 3,000 warriors, and Vassiliev about 4,000 in total. Therefore, the 3,000 Ikhwan could be 1,000, instead. For estimating the numbers of the militia of Khurma, it should be kept in mind that the town only had a population of 4,000. If a half of these were women, and a quarter children and elderly, this – at most – leaves about 1,000 adults able to fight. It is possible that there were 1,000 Ikhwan ′Ataiba at the beginning, and the other 1,100 reinforcements of ibn Bijad. At the end, some 4,100 in all. Perhaps the figure of the Khurmans may seem excessive, but it must be kept in mind that they were fighting for their survival, and that they were already able to defeat Bedouin forces of 800 and 1,700 warriors, so their number would probably have been, at least, similar to them. Glubb, p.59. Almana, pp.63-67, for the details of the battle. They also state that the Hashemites had 30,000 troops – which was impossible. Murphy (p.80), mentions Captain Raho. This author claims not to know who the captain was fighting against, stating that perhaps they were Saudis or Rashidis. From the date and place of death it is evident that it was this battle against the Saudis. Regarding the composition of the Hashemite army, available sources provide no details, but it can be deduced from its composition at the end of the Great War, which we have already reviewed. Thus, despite talking about 5,000 regulars who were joined by tribal contingents, it is more reasonable to think that it was a smaller tribal troop, with a smaller nucleus of regulars, as in 1918. On the other hand, contingents of regulars – the 1st and 2nd Divisions – must be ruled out, because they were with Faysal in the north, and remained with him (the best examples would be above mentioned al-Askari and as-Saad). Abdullah, quoted by Vassiliev, acknowledged the defeat and the casualties suffered, although he claimed that he only had 500 regulars and 850 Bedouins with him, which appears strange considering it is an even smaller contingent than that of his subordinate, ibn Zaid, a year earlier: still, it might have been correct.

Chapter 6

1 Sander, pp.51-53 and 58. Saudi casualty figures are clearly exaggerated: with 1,600 soldiers lost, the Ikhwan would have been annihilated and could not have threatened Kuwait afterwards. Therefore, the estimate for Saud's losses is based on the number of known Kuwaiti casualties (and Kuwaitis won this battle), multiplied by two or three. Notably, Vassiliev (p.254), speaks of 4,000 Ikhwan.

Chapter 7

1 Headley, 'Asir', *Encyclopaedia of Islam*.
2 Sander, pp.53-55. Almana, pp.67-70 for ibn Mussaud. Vassiliev, p.260.

Chapter 8

1 Sander (pp.55-57) is the sole source to provide more details of this operation. The history of Mutluq, also in Sander at p.181. Glubb (pp.59-60), mentions the assassination of ibn Rashid in 1920. Almana, pp.58-59. Vassiliev, pp.254-255. Al Rasheed, p.230.
2 As the reader will notice, the flag of the modern-day Kingdom of Saudi Arabia, comprises only one sword: the one representing 'Justice'. There are no two -swords representing Nejd and Hejaz. However, from 1913 to 1921, the Saudi flag included two crossed swords – one for Nejd, and one for Hasa. Therefore, two swords were initially chosen by ibn Saud as a symbol for his territories. Then, from 1921 and again from 1926, the Saudi flag had only one sword, despite being the flag of Nejd, and then the flag of Nejd and Hejaz: it is probable that the meaning of 'justice' is dating to this period. Nevertheless, since 1938, then in 1953, 1964 and 1973, the Royal Flag, the Royal Standard and the Royal Banner of the King, had again two crossed swords, probably meaning that the Saudi family were the Kings of two kingdoms by conquest, Hejaz and Nejd.

ABOUT THE AUTHOR

Javier G. de Gabiola lives in Madrid and is a practicing lawyer as head of Southern Europe for a US company. Passionate about history and military conflicts of all eras, he has published more than 60 articles in Aventura de la Historia, Muy Historia, Clío, Historia de Iberia Vieja, Desperta Ferro, Historia y Vida, Mundo Medieval, Medievalia, Aviation History, Medieval Warfare, Medieval World, Ancient Warfare, and Autonomous University of Mexico. He is the author of six volumes in English with Helion, such as The Paulista War Vol 1 and 2, The Rif War Vol 1 and 2, The Spanish Passion, and The Swords of Saud Vol 1, and he is now preparing Reds and Blues, about the Spanish Civil War, in several volumes. He has participated also in several Spanish radio programs as África Today in Radio Intercontinental, or Hoy por Hoy in Cadena Ser, both to talk about the Rif War; in La Rosa de los Vientos about the Tercios and the Wars of Spain in Florida; in Istopia Historia, about Blas de Lezo; and in Ágora Historia, about the War of "Gabo" (García Márquez). His other hobbies are cinema, art history, astronomy, travel and the design of board games in which he reproduces several of the military topics studied by him, of which he has published three in the United States and one in Spain.